THE DANDELION CELEBRATION
A Guide to Unexpected Cuisine

By

Peter A. Gail, Ph.D.

Goosefoot Acres Press
CLEVELAND, OHIO

ISBN 1-879863-51-0

Cover and illustrations by Robert Tubbesing
Photo on page 46 by Breitenbach Wineries, Dover, Ohio
Other photos by Peter A. Gail

Published by:

Goosefoot Acres Press
Division of Goosefoot Acres, Inc.
P.O. Box 18016
Cleveland, OH 44118-0016
(216) 932-2145

Library of Congress Cataloging-in-Publication Data

Gail, Peter A., 1939—
    The dandelion celebration : a guide to un-
expected cuisine / by Peter A. Gail.
        p.   cm.
    Originally published under title: On the
trail of the yellow-flowered earth nail, a
dandelion sampler, 1990.
    Includes bibliographical references (p.
[141]-151) and index.
    ISBN 1-879863-51-0 : $10.95
    1. Cookery (Dandelions) 2. Dandelions. I.
Gail, Peter A. On the trail of the yellow-
flowered earth nail, a dandelion sampler.
II. Title.
TX803.D34G35   1994   94-2408
641.6'551--dc20   CIP

10 8 6 4 2 3 5 7 9

To **Agnes Mare,**

long since departed from this life, who taught me at a very young age that there was great value in weeds.

About The Author

Dr. Peter A. Gail, Director of Goosefoot Acres Center for Wild Vegetable Research and Education, earned degrees in Biology and Botany from California State Polytechnic University and Claremont Graduate School and his Ph.D. in Plant Ecology from Rutgers University. Until 1988 he was Associate Professor of Urban and Environmental Studies at Cleveland State University where he lectured and wrote about food and medicinal uses of backyard weeds. Wild vegetable foraging was part of his courses.

For the past 25 years, Dr. Gail has researched recipes and folklore on wild plant use by people throughout the world. He has collected over 3,000 recipes for 105 wild plants, including over 600 for dandelions. He began eating weeds as a young boy after a friend introduced Gail's family to them.

Dr. Gail shares his research and personal experiences through workshops, books, and articles. He is Contributing Editor and columnist for *Business of Herbs,* an international journal for herb growers and marketers. He also writes for the Cleveland *Plain Dealer*, *The Herb Quarterly*, *Herban Lifestyles*, *Herb Companion*, *Wild Food Forum*, *Veggie Digest*, and *Ohio Week*.

Dr. Gail has been married for 33 years and has three children.

Acknowledgments

The information in this book has been collected over the past twenty years with the help of people from all over the world who have shared their stories and recipes. This includes my students who seriously questioned my sanity when I asked them to interview their elderly relatives for dandelion recipes and stories but who were amazed by what they learned. Some of those students, including Cindy Julius, Sheri Gates, and Donna Waldron, devoted long hours to organize the information and enter the recipes in the computer. Bob Tubbesing, my friend, foraging colleague, and collaborator in the dissemination of wild food information, created the cover art. Irma Bartell Dugan, former Garden Editor for the Cleveland *Plain Dealer*, encouraged me to start writing several years ago and Iris Bailin, former Food Editor of the *Plain Dealer*, enthusiastically pushed me along. Dr. James Duke, Steven Foster, Dr. Ed Alstadt, Christopher Hobbs, Portia Meares, and Paula and David Oliver all provided valuable comments and suggestions. This book would not have been possible without the contributions of these people, and I thank them all.

I am also grateful to those dandelion growers, processors, and sellers who have contributed their experience, recipes, anecdotes, folklore, and valuable information which has helped me better understand the value of the remarkable dandelion.

Ann Marie Stockmaster has been and continues to be my faithful, critical, and indispensable associate in preparing this and all our books, as well as a good sport throughout our continuing dandelion adventures. Her talent, insight, devotion, and effort are what keep our production activities on track.

From the very beginning and to this day, my dear wife, Wilma, and our children, Karin, Kevin, and Kori, have willingly and enthusiastically tasted, tested, and thrived off of many foraging trips and kitchen experiments. My son-in-law, Dominic Reale, has been a willing participant, too, inventing the **Dandelion Coffee Ice Cream** recipe in Chapter 8. My family's culinary interest and immeasurable patience through the years have helped transform my dream into the reality of this book.

Every effort has been made to acknowledge all those who have contributed to this book at the point of their contribution. Any omissions or errors, in either fact or attribution, are inadvertent. Those called to my attention will be corrected in subsequent editions.

Preface

When many people consider celebrating dandelions, they do so in much the same spirit as one celebrates overstayed house guests — the party begins once they're gone! But the dandelion, routinely thought of as "lawn enemy number one," is welcomed and celebrated around the world as both a food and medicine. The book in your hands is what I hope will be the first step in transforming American misperceptions of dandelions.

Dandelions are about the best wild vegetable resource in the world. They are free, abundant, nutritious, and very palatable when collected at the right time, in the right way, and prepared properly.

Many "backyard weeds," like dandelions, are true vegetables which were long ago transported to America by immigrants and cultivated for food. Most gradually fell out of favor but still thrive in our gardens and lawns, waiting to be rediscovered and added to our menus.

Numerous how-to books introduce edible wild plants. A few, such as the *Goosefoot Acres Volunteer Vegetable Sampler — Recipes for Backyard Weeds*, focus on common backyard and garden weeds. **The Dandelion Celebration** is one of the first books devoted to exploring the attributes and uses of a single plant species. It is the first in a series of such books to be published by Goosefoot Acres Press. I invite you to try these "volunteer vegetables" with curious taste buds and an open mind. What you discover will surprise and delight you.

Information on the purported medical attributes of dandelions is being passed on to you for information only. I am not a medical doctor and neither advocate nor prescribe dandelions or dandelion products for any medical purpose. If you know or suspect that you have specific illnesses, chronic conditions, or food-related or other allergies, contact your physician for medical advice. It is very important that you consult with your doctor when ill and follow his/her recommendations. Your doctor can advise you whether dandelion remedies are for you. Some of the recipes contained in this book may be inappropriate for persons suffering from certain physical conditions. I assume no liability for omissions or for the use or misuse of the information contained in this book.

If, after reading this book and experimenting with the recipes, you find that dandelions aren't for you, either share the book with a friend who might enjoy them, or, if it is still in saleable condition, send it back for a refund. We want you to be happy.

Please send comments, additions, and other suggestions to **Peter A. Gail, Ph.D., Goosefoot Acres Center for Wild Vegetable Research and Education, P.O. Box 18016, Cleveland Heights, OH 44118.**

Peter A. Gail, Ph.D.
March, 1994

Contents

Chapter 1

Can Any Good
Come From a Dandelion?

What do James Beard, Craig Claiborne, The Frugal Gourmet, Bert Greene, and the U.S. Government all have in common?

Can't guess? Well, believe it or not, they all consider **dandelions**, those pernicious weeds which you work so hard to get rid of, to be **food**, and extremely good food at that. In fact, James Beard, the celebrated American chef and author, was so fond of them that he featured blanched dandelion crowns *au gratin* on the menu of the First Conference on Gastronomy at the founding of the American Institute on Wine and Food (Hampstead, 1988).

The British, Russians, and Europeans generally love dandelions. They eat, drink, and make money from them in innumerable ways. The Chinese (some of whom call them **yellow-flowered earth nails** or *Huang-hua-tii-ting*) revere dandelions and consider them one of the six most important plants in their herbal medicine chest.

Most Americans, however, with the exception of children and other romantics who frolic in the yellow seas of springtime, making crowns and chains and trying to decide who likes butter, generally wish they'd go away and die!

It seems that many of us possess a conscious *will not to believe* anything good about this remarkable harbinger of spring which, by its ubiquity and persistence, make it the most recognized **and** most hated of all "weeds." If you are one of those people who feel this way about dandelions, I give you a challenge. This year, as you stand at the door contemplating how much herbicide it will take to eradicate dandelions from your life, consider these facts:

- Dandelions, under the name "Ciccoria," are almost the Italian national dish. Italians eat them in salads, with beans, and with spaghetti. They put them on pizza and even bake them into bread! Dandelions are gourmet fare to the French, who do remarkable things with their beloved "Pissenlit." They are also popular with many New Englanders, the Pennsylvania Dutch, Southern Appalachians and Blacks, and people representing some 40 other different nationality and cultural groups, including the English, Germans, Koreans, Lebanese, Greeks, and Armenians.

- About *one out of every four* American cookbooks contains recipes for dandelions. People are incredulous when I take them to their kitchen bookshelf, open **their** cookbooks, and show them the recipes. Their typical response? "They may be in there, but you'll never catch *me* eatin' 'em!"

- According to the U.S. Department of Agriculture Handbook No. 8, *Composition of Foods* (the official dictator of what *is* and what *is not* food in the United States), dandelions rank ahead of both broccoli and spinach in nutritional value (See Chapter 3).

- The combination of nutrients and various curatives make dandelions a favored remedy for many ills (See Chapter 3).

- Growing and selling dandelion greens and roots and packaging various dandelion-based herbal preparations is a multi-million dollar international industry (See Chapter 4).

But the fact which will probably surprise you most is that, while most Americans are spending millions to eradicate dandelions from their yards, other Americans are *buying* dandelion seeds from Nichols, Stokes, The Cook's Garden, and other seed houses. While *you* are destroying them, *they* are planting them!

For what it is worth, dandelions are also a favorite hog and poultry food and are used to feed silkworms when mulberry leaves are scarce! Max Brighton, a potato farmer and rancher from Burleigh, Idaho, told me that his cows and horses love dandelions, but if the cows are allowed to eat them while they are flowering, it makes the milk bitter. Hobbs (1985) reported on a study in the *Canadian Journal of Animal Science* which found dandelion to be a favorite food plant of deer and second only to the common horsetail (*Equisetum arvense*) in digestibility among forage plants. For bird lovers, dandelion seeds attract purple finches. Our gerbils go wild over them!

They are favored by other animals as well. Mrs. Frances Barman, a 91-year-old Slovenian lady who lives in Cleveland, Ohio, reported that while collecting dandelions in a field, she was approached by a large German shepherd dog who began eating the dandelions out of her basket. According to Frances, "We had quite a discussion before I finally convinced him that those dandelions were *mine* and he went on his way."

Dandelions are inherently bitter. You need to know that from the start. But, because they are so nutritious and have so many potential health-giving properties, it is worth finding a way to mask or reduce the bitterness so that you may benefit from the advantages. Fortunately, this is easy to do.

Currently, I have over 600 recipes for dandelions representing some 42 different ethnic sources. While many come from general, ethnic, and regional cookbooks, the best have been handed down by word-of-mouth through the generations in ethnic households and are being published here for the first time. This sampler contains over 70 recipes selected from that collection.

I recognize that most of you who are reading this are doing so voluntarily and are both open-minded and seriously interested in doing something constructive with your dandelions. If you weren't, you wouldn't have picked up this book in the first place. But if you are one of the millions who are contemplating whether to spend $60 on do-it-yourself weed killers and do the back-breaking work yourself or to drop $120 on a professional lawn treatment service and let them do the job, and whose neighbor, in desperation, has thrust this book into your hands, stop! Sit back in your most comfortable easy chair and immerse yourself in at least the first three or four chapters. Then you can make an educated decision about what to do with that bounteous harvest which spreads before you.

Chapter 2

From Whence They Came And By Whom

Holly Shimazu, assistant to the Executive Director of the U.S. Botanic Garden in Washington D.C., tells about a lady who was so fascinated by the beauty of the dandelion that she chose the most perfect specimen she could find in her lawn, transplanted it to the finest, most fertile spot in her garden, and nurtured it. She watered it, sunned it, fed it, prayed over it and loved it. Then she entered it in the local flower show. It won first prize! When she went to retrieve it for the trip back home, *someone had stolen it*! How important perspective and publicity are in establishing a perception of value.

In fact, during the 19th century, growing, showing, and consuming dandelions were common pursuits in both Europe and the United States. Louis Noisette, in his *Manuel du Jardinier* (1829) told how to grow dandelions. In 1871, Fearing Burr, the prominent American horticulturist, exhibited four varieties of dandelions at the Massachusetts Horticultural Society show — the French large-leaved, the French thick-leaved, the red-seeded and the American Improved. In 1879, French horticulturalists listed five varieties in their catalogs, and by 1881, two varieties were being listed in United States seed catalogs. In 1884, a Mr. Corey, of Brookline, Massachusetts, was growing dandelions from seed for sale on the Boston market.

Dandelions have long been used by humans as medicine and food. Biblical scholars believe that the bitter herbs referred to in Exodus 12:8 and Numbers 9:11 were weedy, herbaceous salad plants which included dandelions (Core, n.d.).

The earliest certain reference to the use of dandelions as medicine is in Avicenna's *Herbal of Mittlealters*, a product of the great Arabian school of medicine in the 11th century (Hobbs, 1985). Since at least medieval times, dandelions have been used throughout Europe, the British Isles, and Russia as a popular salad green and potherb.

Dandelions even figure in Greek mythology, where it is reported that the hero, Theseus, having been fed dandelions for thirty days by the moon goddess Hecate, became powerful enough to kill the notorious Minotaur, the half man-half bull which ate young men and maidens.

Botanically, the dandelion is a member of the plant family *Compositae* (*Asteraceae*). Its relatives include sunflowers, asters, marigolds, and daisies as well as such vegetables as lettuce, endive, chicory, and artichokes. It is perennial and produces long taproots which penetrate deep, allowing it to absorb great quantities of nutrients and trace minerals from various soil strata. Its strap-shaped leaves, which can grow 10" to 12" long in cultivation, form a rosette of leaves clustered tightly along a short stem. Leaves tend to be broader at the top and taper to the base and are possessed of deep, ragged "teeth" which inspired the French to call the plant "dent de lion" (lion's tooth), from which the name dandelion is derived. Hollow flower stems, each bearing a single flower and containing a bitter, milky, latex-filled sap, rise from the rosette. (See diagram on page 56). The Russian dandelion, *Taraxacum koksaghyuz*, was cultivated for rubber in the Soviet Union, and small quantities of rubber were made from the sap of the common dandelion in the United States during World War II. A yellow-flowered inflorescence 1" or more in diameter (which is made up of many little individual flowers, each with a single strap shaped group of five fused petals) sits atop this stem in spring, The fruit head, which follows the flower, is the ball-shaped cluster of small, one-seeded fruits, each topped with its own "parachute" of fine tufted hairs that the wind carries where it will.

The most delightful description of this remarkable plant I have ever encountered was written by John Parkinson, the apothecary of London and the King's Herbarist, in *Theatrum Botanicum - The Theatre of Plants or An Universall and Compleate Herball*, in 1640. I can't resist sharing it!

> Our common dandelion is well knowne to have many long and deeply gashed leaves lying on the ground round about the head of the roote, the ends of each gash or jagge on both sides looking downward to the roote againe, the middle ribbe being white which being broken yeeld abundance of bitter milke, but the

> roote much more from among the leaves
> which alwayes abide greene, arise many
> slender weake naked foote stalkes, rather
> than stalkes, every one of them being at
> the toppe one large yellow flower, consist-
> ing of many rowes of yellow leaves, broad
> at the pointes and nicked in with a deep
> spot of yellow in the middle which, grow-
> ing ripe, the greene husk wherein the
> flower stood turneth it selfe downe to the
> stalke, and the head of downe becommeth
> as round as a ball with long reddish seede
> underneath bearing apart of the downe
> on the head of every one which together
> is blowne away with the wind, or with the
> blast of ones mouth may be blowne away
> at once, the roote groweth downewards
> exceeding deepe, which being broken off
> within the ground will, notwithstanding,
> shoote forth anew againe and will hardly
> be destroyed where it hath once taken
> deepe rooting in the ground.

And that *all in one sentence*, mind you! Writing styles, not to mention spelling, have certainly changed in 350 years, haven't they?

Dandelions are thought by some to have originat- ed around Greece and by others in the Northern Hima- layas, where some 75 different species still exist today. Wherever they originated, the immigration of dandelions to America is shrouded in conflicting claims. The earli- est is that they arrived with the Vikings in 1000 A.D.; the latest is the claim (Fulweiler, n.d.) that they arrived in Massachusetts as contaminants in vegetable seed packets in the 19th century. Another source contends that they first came on the Mayflower, citing that a 1630 inventory of the flora of Plymouth Colony turned up no dandelions, but by 1680 they were everywhere around the colony. There are also accounts of dandelions being eaten raw and cooked by the Digger Indians of Colorado and the Apaches of Arizona and used as medicine by the Kiowas and Chippewas, but these date from the late 19th century after the dandelion had already been established in America.

If we are to believe the many conflicting claims in the historical record, we must conclude that dandelions have come to us again and again over the years on ships carrying Italian, German, French, Oriental, Greek, Lebanese, Armenian, and just about every other immigrant to arrive on American shores.

After arriving, dandelions spread over the continent much faster than the colonists. Their rapid advance was enhanced by their ability to produce millions of seeds without requiring pollination through a process called *apomixis*. Special cells in the ovule, which don't undergo the normal reduction in chromosome number typical of sexual reproduction, produce embryos identical to those of the parent plant. These clones then take to the air in their little parachutes and drop to the ground where the wind lets them off, which can be many miles away. Once established, their root systems take over and spread the plant even more widely.

Whereas some plants protect themselves from extinction by thorns or toxic chemicals, others, including popular forage plants like the dandelion, simply do it by growing faster than they are consumed, regrowing from the same roots over and over, and acclimating to the lawnmower by flowering, fruiting, and dispersing their seeds faster and at a much lower height than they would under normal conditions.

In addition to their attractiveness to humans for food and medicine, dandelions are, overall, ecological "good guys." They convert nitrogen to nitrates in the soil, and bring long-buried soil nutrients to the surface. They are so effective at depleting the soil of nutrients that it is difficult for plants living around them to remain healthy as long as the dandelions are alive. Dead dandelions, however, are terrific soil enrichers. A fine liquid fertilizer can be made by immersing a handful of leaves in a pint of water, bringing it to a boil, covering it, and allowing it to cool. After it is cooled, strain the liquid off, dilute with four parts of water, add a soup spoonful of any liquid soap (not detergent) and use immediately as a leaf spray.

Dandelions are a mixed blessing, however, to orchard owners. On the one side, they exude ethylene which assists in the ripening of fruit, but, on the other, bees like dandelion pollen so well that they can be distracted from pollinating fruit trees!

Dandelions are a favored spring vegetable of rural New England farmers and fishermen, Mennonites, Amish, and other Pennsylvania Dutch, as well as many other rural folks in the East, Midwest, and South. I know several New England fishermen who get such cravings for dandelion greens that they can hardly wait for spring. They look upon these greens as a tonic which purges winter toxins from the bloodstream and prepares farmer and fisherman alike for the working season. It is this diuretic property which has resulted in several common names in France and England, such as "pissenlit" and "piss-a-bed" which warn heavy sleepers not to feast too heavily on dandelions before going to bed!

Italians everywhere harvest dandelion greens in spring and blanch and freeze them to eat throughout the year. The Portuguese like them in mid-summer when they are most bitter. Koreans are the primary customer for dandelions in Philadelphia. In Los Angeles, it's the Armenians, Greeks, and Italians. An old Italian told a friend of mine that when dandelions get more bitter as the summer progresses, they just add more pepper. That way they can eat them all summer long.

There is a rich folklore surrounding dandelions, both here and abroad. Stories include those about:

- a woman in Denver, around the turn of the century, who went so far as to have unsuspecting boys arrested for trampling the dandelions which she had lovingly brought with her from the East (Harris, 1961).

- how farm wives in small Italian villages, during World War II when anemia was widespread, would put a pot of dandelion soup on their window sills for poor passersby to eat to improve their blood.

- how dandelions almost became extinct in the British Isles during the 1950's, prompting the founding of a "Save the Dandelions" society (Nyerges). A similar

"Society for the Preservation of Dandelions" with some 400 members flourished in the United States until 1990.

- how dandelions saved the Minorcans from starvation when locusts destroyed their crops and sustained displaced persons during and after World War II until the Marshall Plan was able to restore stability to Europe. People in displaced person camps supplemented their thin potato soup by foraging wild greens, chief among which were dandelions.

- the French and others bring dandelion roots indoors over winter so that they will have greens all winter long (See Chapter 8).

- John Breisch, a former NASA research engineer, who grew up in a Pennsylvania German community, reported that every spring the folks in his neighborhood would rejoice when the dandelions came up. "They would eat dandelions until they looked like them," he said. "When you had dandelion pie at home, that was living!" They drank the juice, which they felt was good medicine for everyone. They made a poultice out of the crushed leaves which was put on arthritis, cuts, earaches, and burns. "Burns," he says, "would fight back as hard as they could, but finally succumbed to the dandelion poultice." Whatever couldn't be cured with the poultice would be cured by the juice! Each spring, his Lutheran church would devote a Sunday to the celebration of the emergence of the dandelion as a great blessing from God.

Stories about families and communities having annual dandelion feasts are numerous. The Wright family in Fremont, Ohio, for example, gathers from all over the Midwest each spring to feed on steamed dandelion greens, vinegar, and bacon chunks spooned over mashed potatoes. For many years, Vineland, New Jersey has hosted an annual Dandelion Dinner which is publicized nationally and draws more visitors than town-folks (see page 79) and White Sulphur Springs, West Virginia sponsors an annual dandelion festival, complete with parade and a dandelion wine-tasting contest.

Other stories which relate to the health benefits of dandelions are in Chapter 3.

A last story illustrates how thoroughly we are conditioned not to notice dandelions in any context other than as weeds. One afternoon I was photographing a dandelion display in a west-side Cleveland supermarket when I was approached by a nice, elderly lady who asked what I was doing. "I'm photographing this display of dandelion greens," I said, to which she responded with great surprise, "I've shopped here for ten years and have never seen dandelions in the store before!" It turned out that she had grown up on dandelions in her native Pennsylvania as a member of a Pennsylvania Dutch family, had missed the annual spring dandelion ritual, and was delighted to have a source of dandelions from which to make her Buttermilk Dandelion Gravy. She bought two big bunches and gave me the recipe. You will find it on page 83.

I have been studying dandelions for over twenty years, and have discovered that, while little has been written about them in any one place, the oral folklore is rich. Everywhere I go I learn something new about dandelions. Every now and then, when I brashly claim to be something of an authority on the subject, I am humbled and enriched by a barrage of new information and stories about the plant which I had never heard before. I expect that this will go on as long as I seek information on dandelions. Hopefully, this book will open the door for you to share your stories and recipes with me, so that one day I will truly be able to say that I know most of what there is to know about this remarkable plant. Please send them to the address listed in the front of this book.

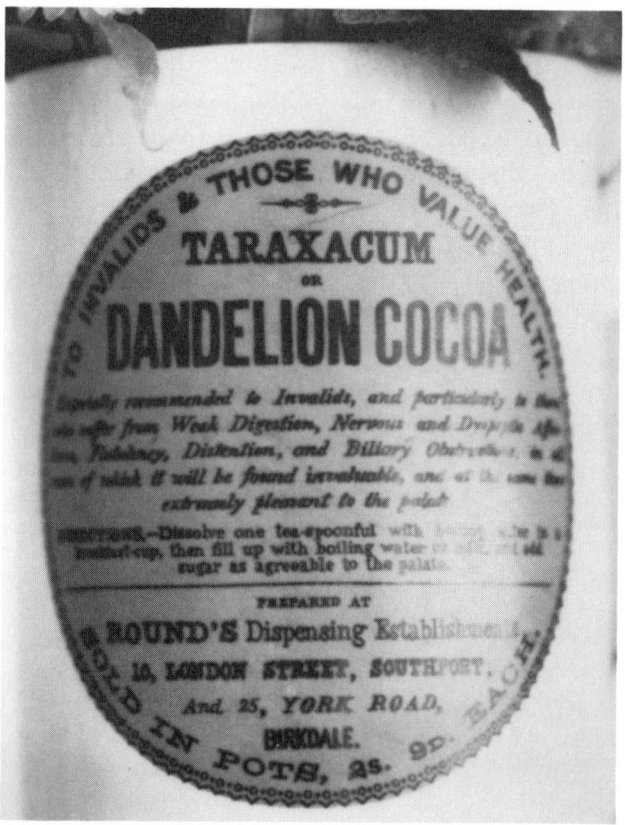

Chapter 3

The Health Benefits of Dandelions

Suppose your doctor tells you, on your next visit, that a miracle drug which he has just discovered, when eaten as a part of your daily diet could, depending on the peculiarities of your body chemistry:

- **prevent or cure liver diseases, such as hepatitis, cirrhosis or jaundice;**

- **act as a tonic and gentle diuretic to purify your blood, cleanse your system, dissolve kidney stones, and otherwise improve gastro-intestinal health;**

- **assist in weight reduction;**

- **improve your vision;**

- **cleanse your skin and eliminate acne;**

- **improve your bowel function, working equally well to relieve both constipation and diarrhea;**

- **prevent (or lower) high blood pressure;**

- **prevent or cure anemia;**

- **lower your serum cholesterol by as much as half;**

- **eliminate or drastically reduce acid indigestion and gas buildup by cutting the heaviness of fatty foods;**

- **prevent or cure various forms of cancer; and**

- **prevent or help control diabetes.**

At the same time, this "miracle medicine" would have no negative side effects and selectively act on only what ails you. If he gave you a prescription for this miracle medicine, would you use it religiously, first to solve whatever the problem is and then consistently for preventive body maintenance?

All the above curative functions, and more, have been attributed to the dandelion, scientifically known as *Taraxacum officinale*, the "official remedy for disorders." The dandelion is so well respected, in fact, that it appeared in the U.S. *National Formulary* until 1960, and in the pharmacopoeias of Hungary, Poland, Switzerland, and the countries formerly included in the Soviet Union. Furthermore, the dandelion is one of the top six herbs in the Chinese herbal medicine chest.

According to the USDA Bulletin No. 8, *Composition of Foods* (Haytowitz and Matthews, 1984), dandelions rank ahead of both broccoli and spinach in overall nutritional value. Minnich, in *Gardening for Better Nutrition* (1983), ranks them, out of **all** vegetables, including grains, seeds, and greens, as tied for ninth best.

Comparative nutritional characteristics of dandelions and other vegetables, taken from the USDA data, are presented in Table 1.

NUTRITIONAL COMPARISONS BETWEEN WILD AND DOMESTIC VEGETABLES
(Food Value per 100 gram [3.53 oz.] serving)

Vegetable		Cal.	Prot. gm	Fat gm	CHO Tot. gm	Fib gm	Ca mg	P mg	Fe mg	Na mg	Mg mg	K mg	A IU	Thia mg	Ribo mg	Nia mg	C mg	Water %
WILD																		
Amaranth	(r)	36	3.5	0.5	6.5	1.3	267	67	3.9	--	--	411	6100	.08	.16	1.4	80	86.9
Dandelion	(r)	45	2.7	0.7	9.2	1.6	187	66	3.1	76	284	397	14000	.19	.26		35	85.6
	(c)	33	2.0	0.6	6.4	1.3	140	42	1.8	44	--	232	11700	.13	.16		18	89.2
Lambsqtrs	(r)	43	4.2	0.8	7.3	2.1	309	72	1.2	--	--	--	11600	.16	.44	1.2	80	84.3
	(c)	32	3.2	0.7	5.0	1.8	258	45	0.7	--	--	--	9700	.10	.26	0.9	37	88.9
DOMESTIC																		
Broccoli	(r)	32	3.6	0.3	5.9	1.5	103	78	1.1	15	24	382	2500	.10	.23	0.9	113	89.1
	(c)	26	3.1	0.3	5.9	1.5	88	62	0.8	10	--	267	2500	.09	.20	0.8	90	91.3
Collard	(r)	45	4.8	0.8	7.5	1.2	250	82	1.5	--	57	450	9300	.16	.31	1.7	152	85.3
	(c)	33	3.6	0.7	5.1	1.0	188	52	0.8	--	--	262	7800	.11	.20	1.2	76	86.9
Spinach	(r)	26	3.2	0.3	4.3	0.6	93	51	3.1	71	88	470	8100	.10	.20	0.6	51	90.7
	(c)	23	3.0	0.3	3.6	0.6	93	38	2.2	50	--	324	8100	.07	.14	0.5	28	92.0
Lettuce (Rom)		18	1.3	0.3	3.5	0.7	68	25	1.4	9	--	264	1900	.05	.08	0.4	18	94.0
Lettuce (ice)		13	0.9	0.1	2.9	0.5	20	22	0.5	9	11	175	330	.06	.06	0.3	6	96.0
USRDA			45	--	--	--	1000	1000	18.0	3000	400	2000	5000	1.5	1.7	20.0	60	--

Legend: (r) = raw; (c) = cooked; USRDA = U.S. Recommended Daily Allowance; Cal = Calories; Prot = Protein; CHO = Carbohydrates; Fib = Fiber; Ca = Calcium; P = Phosphorus; Fe = Iron; Na = Sodium; Mg = Magnesium; K = Potassium; A (IU) = Vitamin A in international units; Thia = Thiamin (Vit. B1); Ribo = Riboflavin (Vit. B2); C = Vitamin C; mg. = milligrams; gm = grams
Reference values (100 gm portions): Potassium - Banana, 370 mg.; Vitamin C - Oranges, 40-45 mg. (juice), 50-60 mg. (fruit), acerola (rose hips) - 1300 mg.
Reference weights: 100 gm = 3.52 oz; 100 gm x 4.54 = 1 lb; 454 gm. = 1 lb. 1 oz = 28.35 gm
(Source: American Heart Assn. Dietary Guidelines for Healthy American Adults. #71-1003, 1992 Report of Joint National Comm. on Dietary Evaluation and Treatment of High Blood Pressure. Haytowitz and Matthews, 1984 Composition of Foods. Agricultural Handbook #8-11, U.S. Department of Agriculture).

TABLE 1

The top nine vegetables, based on those listed in *Composition of Foods*, rank-ordered based on relative quantity of nutrients present in each, are presented in Table 2, with two varieties of lettuce included for comparison:

TABLE 2

NUTRITIONAL COMPARISON OF ELEVEN LEAFY GREEN VEGETABLES
(Ranked in order of most to least nutritious)

Food Value per 100 gram [3.53 oz.] serving

Vegetable	Protein gm.	Fiber gm.	Calcium mg.	Phosphorus mg.	Iron mg.	Postassium mg.	Vit. A IU	Thiamin mg.	Riboflavin mg.	Niacin mg.	Vit. C mg.
Lambsquarters*	4.3	2.1	309	72	1.2	--	11600	.16	.44	1.2	80
Collards	4.8	1.2	250	82	1.5	450	9300	.16	.31	1.7	152
Amaranth	3.5	1.3	267	67	3.9	411	6100	.08	.16	1.4	80
Dandelions	2.7	1.6	187	66	3.1	397	14000	.19	.26		35
Broccoli	3.6	1.5	103	78	1.1	382	2500	.10	.23	0.9	113
Spinach	3.2	0.6	93	51	3.1	470	8100	.10	.20	0.6	51
Mustard	3.0	1.1	183	50	3.0	377	7000	.11	.22	0.8	97
Beet Greens	2.2	1.3	119	40	3.3	570	6100	.10	.22	0.9	30
Turnip Greens	1.5	0.8	190	42	1.1	296	7600	.07	.10	0.6	60
Lettuce (Rom)	1.3	0.7	68	25	1.4	264	1900	.05	.08	0.4	18
Lettuce (Ice)	0.9	0.5	20	22	0.5	175	330	.06	.06	0.3	6

(Source: Haytowitz and Matthews, 1984 <u>Composition of Foods</u>. Agricultural Handbook #8-11, U.S. Department of Agriculture).

* boldface indicates common "weeds"

Please note that according to this analysis, three of the top five vegetables are common "weeds" — **lambsquarters, amaranth (pigweed) and dandelions! Collard** is the only domestic green to break into the top four, and **broccoli**, touted by many as nature's ultimate vitamin pill, ranks only fifth, just ahead of **spinach**.

Table 3 presents the percent of the recommended daily allowance of each nutrient that a 3.5 oz. serving of each of these five vegetables would supply:

PERCENT OF RECOMMENDED DAILY ALLOWANCE OF BASIC NUTRIENTS
IN FIVE MOST-NUTRITIOUS GREEN VEGETABLES
(Food Value per 100 gram [3.53 oz.] serving)

All values, except fiber, expressed in percentage of Recommended Daily Allowance

Vegetable	Prot.	Fat*	CHO Tot.*	Fib*	Ca	P	Fe	Na	Mg	K	A	Thia	Ribo	Nia	C
Lambsquarters	10	.8	7.3	2.1	31	7	7	--	--	--	232	11	26	6	133
Collard	11	.8	7.5	1.2	25	8	8	--	14	22	186	11	18	9	253
Dandelions	6	.7	9.2	1.6	19	7	17	3	71	20	280	13	15	--	58
Amaranth	8	.5	6.5	1.3	27	7	22	--	--	20	122	5	9	7	133
Broccoli	8	.3	5.9	1.5	10	8	6	1	6	19	50	7	14	5	188

Legend: Prot = Protein; CHO = Carbohydrates; Fib = Fiber; Ca = Calcium; P = Phosphorus; Fe = Iron; Na = Sodium; Mg = Magnesium; K = Potassium; A (IU) = Vitamin A in international units; Thia = Thiamin (Vit. B1); Ribo = Riboflavin (Vit. B2); C = Vitamin C

* No RDA is established for fiber, fat or total carbohydrates. Value is expressed in grams present in 100 grams of fresh material.

Dandelions rank **first** in magnesium, Vitamin A, total carbohydrates and thiamine, second in fiber, iron, sodium and potassium; third in fat and riboflavin, fourth in phosphorus and calcium and fifth in Vitamin C and protein.

Source: Federal Extension Service, Key Nutrients. U.S. Dept. of Agriculture, Nutrients and Food for Health. American Heart Assn. Dietary Guidelines for Healthy American Adults. #71-1003, 1992 Report of Joint National Comm. on Dietary Evaluation and Treatment of High Blood Pressure. Haytowitz and Matthews, 1984 Composition of Foods. Agricultural Handbook #8-11, U.S. Department of Agriculture.

TABLE 3

According to the University of California School of Public Health's *Wellness Letter* (February, 1990), dandelions are nature's richest vegetable source of beta-carotene, the substance which the body converts into Vitamin A. (Unlike synthetically produced Vitamin A supplements, beta-carotene is non-toxic in large doses because the body regulates its conversion to Vitamin A). They contain 8.4 mg. of beta-carotene per 10 gm., compared to carrots, which contain 6.1 mg./10 gm., as well as being particularly rich in fiber, potassium, iron, calcium, magnesium, phosphorus, and the B vitamins (thiamine and riboflavin).

These figures represent only those published by the USDA. Studies in Russia and Eastern Europe by Gerasimova, Racz, Vogel, and Marei as reported in Hobbs (1985) indicated that dandelions are also rich in micronutrients such as copper, cobalt, zinc, boron, and molybdenum, as well as Vitamin D.

Much of what is claimed that dandelions can do to promote good health could result from nutritional richness alone. Vogel considers the sodium in dandelions important in reducing inflammations of the liver. Gerasimova, the Russian chemist who analyzed the dandelion for, among other things, trace minerals, stated that "dandelion [is] an example of a harmonious combination of trace elements, vitamins and other biologically active substances in ratios optimal for a human organism" (Hobbs, 1985).

Recent research, reported in the *Natural Healing and Nutrition Annual, 1989* (Bricklin and Ferguson,

1989) on the value of vitamins and minerals indicates that:

- **Vitamin A** is important in fighting cancers of epithelial tissue, including mouth and lung;

- **Potassium-rich foods**, in adequate quantities, and particularly in balance with **magnesium**, help keep blood pressure down and reduce risks of strokes. (However, **boiling** destroys up to 30% of the potassium in vegetables, so they should be eaten raw, steamed, microwaved, or stir-fried);

- **Fiber** fights diabetes, lowers cholesterol, reduces cancer and heart disease risks, and assists in weight loss. High-fiber vegetables take up lots of room, are low in calories, and slow down digestion so the food stays in the stomach longer and you feel full longer;

- high concentrations of **calcium** build strong bones and can lower blood pressure;

- **B vitamins** help reduce stress.

In addition, **iron** is very important in the prevention of anemia.

From the nutritional standpoint alone, any of the five green vegetables in Tables 2 and 3, as well as others, if included regularly in the diet, would promote excellent health and help prevent bodily malfunctions.

Al Brown, III, a former All-American football player at the University of Dayton and defensive back with the Buffalo Bills, grew up on a diet of mixed greens which included dandelions and entered college lean, trim, and in peak condition. His teammates at the University of Dayton were amazed that a "skinny guy like that" could bench press 300 pounds, which was almost twice his body weight. After three months on training table food, he bloated up so that his mother, when he returned home at Christmas, thought he was sick. After two weeks on greens, he was back in shape again. The feeling of vibrant health is common to all I have interviewed who grew up on a regular diet of dandelion and other wild greens.

Throughout history, dandelions have had a reputation as being effective in promoting weight loss, and laboratory research indicates that there is some support for this reputation. Controlled tests on laboratory mice and rats by Romanian scientists indicated that a loss of up to 30% of body weight in thirty days was possible when the animals were fed an aqueous extract of dandelions with their food. Those on grass extract lost much less. The control group on plain water actually gained weight. The greatest weight loss corresponded to 4 oz. of dandelion per day for a 140 lb. individual.

Several years ago, two friends and I spent a long weekend camping and working in Mercer County, Pennsylvania, living off wild vegetables and fish. I discovered that a single meal of dandelions and other wild vegetables so satisfied my appetite that, even though working hard clearing timber and tending fish seines, I didn't even think about eating until some twenty-four hours later. That was when I first realized that wild vegetables are the natural diet foods — they are so filled with nutrients and fiber that they totally satisfy bodily needs for these elements and the "appestat" has no cause to turn on to indicate hunger.

The concept behind very low calorie diets is the same — put everything the body needs into a small, low-calorie package. When the body has met its needs, the appestat turns off, and the craving for food goes away! Foraging may not be as convenient as fixing a milkshake from a can of powder, but it seems to be at least as effective, probably healthier, and a whole lot cheaper. One of the grand ironies in the whole dandelion story is that there exist in this world folks who spend megabucks on dandelion-destroying chemicals and then $20 or so a week for a particular diet food which contains dandelions and other common backyard weeds in its list of ingredients.

Beyond nutritional richness, however, are the active chemical constituents contained in dandelions which may have specific therapeutic effects on the body. These include, as reported by Hobbs (1985):

- The starch, **inulin**, which converts to **fructose** (fruit sugar) in the presence of cold or hydrochloric acid in the stomach. Fructose forms glycogen in the liver without seeming to require insulin, resulting in a slower blood sugar rise. This makes it of interest to diabetics and hypoglycemics;

- **TOf-CFr**, a glucose polymer similar to lentinan, which Japanese researchers have found to act against cancer cells in laboratory mice. Lentinan is a yeast glucan (glucose polymer) that increases resistance to protozoal and viral infections;

- **Pectin**, which is an anti-diarrheal and also forms ionic complexes with metal ions, may contribute to dandelion's reputation as a blood and gastrointestinal detoxifying herb. Pectin is prescribed regularly in Russia to remove heavy metals and radioactive elements from body tissues. Pectin can also lower cholesterol and, combined with Vitamin C, can lower it even more. Dandelion is a source of both pectin **and** Vitamin C;

- **Apigenin and Luteolin**, two flavonoid glycosides which have been demonstrated to have diuretic, anti-spasmodic, anti-oxidant, and liver protecting actions and properties, and also to strengthen the heart and blood vessels. They also have anti-bacterial and anti-hypoglycemic properties;

- **Gallic Acid,** which is an anti-diarrheal and anti-bacterial;

- **Linoleic and Linolenic Acid,** which are essential fatty acids required by the body to produce prostaglandins that regulate blood pressure and such body processes as immune responses which suppress inflammation. These fatty acids can lower chronic inflammation, such as proliferative arthritis, regulate blood pressure and the menstrual cycle, and prevent platelet aggregation;

- **Choline**, which has been shown to help improve memory;

- **Sesquiterpene compounds** are what make dandelions bitter. These may partly account for the tonic effects of dandelions on digestion, liver, spleen, and gall bladder. They are also highly anti-fungal;

- **Triterpenes,** which may contribute to bile or liver stimulation;

- **Taraxasterol**, which may contribute to liver and gall bladder health.

- In addition, **apigenin, luteolin, and coumestrol** (another chemical present in dandelions) function as estrogen mimics which can have beneficial effects on the female reproductive organs.

These chemicals, individually, are not unique to dandelions, but the combination of them all in one plant, along with high levels of vitamins, minerals, carbohydrates, proteins, and fiber may account for the many claims made regarding the plant.

These claims include the following results of clinical and laboratory research, again, as reported in Hobbs (1985):

- **A doubling of bile output with leaf extracts and a quadrupling of bile output with root extract.** Bile assists with the emulsification, digestion, and absorption of fats, in alkalinizing the intestines and in the prevention of putrefaction. This could explain the effectiveness of dandelion in reducing the effects of fatty foods (acid indigestion and gas buildup);

- **Reduction in serum cholesterol and urine bilirubin** levels by as much as half in humans with severe liver imbalances has been demonstrated by Italian researchers;

- **Diuretic effects** with a strength approaching that of the potent diuretic drug, furosemide, with none of the dangerous side effects, were found by Romanian scientists. Because of its high potassium content, dandelion extract, administered orally, replaces serum potassium electrolytes lost in the urine;

- In 1979, a Japanese patent was granted for a freeze-dried warm water extract of dandelion root for **anti-tumor use.** It was found that administration of the extract markedly inhibited growth of particular carcinoma cells within one week after treatment;

- In studies from 1941 to 1952, the French scientist, Henri Leclerc, demonstrated the effectiveness of dandelion on **chronic liver problems related to bile stones.** He recommended that a beverage made from dandelion roots gathered in late summer to fall (when they are rich in bitter, white milky latex), roasted, and prepared like coffee, should be used for all liver treatments (see page 135);

- In 1956, Chauvin demonstrated the **antibacterial effects of dandelion pollen**, which may validate the centuries-old use of dandelion flowers in Korean folk medicine to cure boils, skin infections, tuberculosis, and edema, and promote blood circulation.

- Witt (1983) recommends dandelion tea to **alleviate the water retention associated with PMS** (pre-menstrual syndrome).

- Duke (1993) reports that dandelion flowers are one of nature's richest sources of lecithin, which has been shown to prevent **cirrhosis of the liver**. "So," he says, "I'd recommend drinking dandelion wine if you like to lift an occasional glass but are worried about getting cirrhosis."

There are many testimonials from those who have benefitted from the use of dandelions in "treating what ails them."

Robert Stickle, an internationally-famous architect, was diagnosed as having a malignant melanoma and was given, after radical surgery had not halted its spread, less than two years to live. He said, in a letter to Jeff Zullo, president of the Society for the Promotion of Dandelions, (June 23, 1986):

> I went on a search for the answer to my mortal problem, and [discovered] that perhaps it was a nutritional dilemma.... To me, cancer is primarily a liver failure manifestation. (Italians are very concerned about problems of the 'fegato'). [I discovered that] the cancer rate in native Italians is very low among the farming population (paesanos). When they get affluent and move to the city, it's the same as the rest of civilized man. Paesanos eat dandelions, make brew from the

roots, and are healthy, often living to over
100 years.

He stated that he began eating dandelion salad every
day, and his improvement confounded the doctors.
When he wrote the letter in 1986, 18 years had passed
and there had been no recurrence of the melanoma.

A benefit which comes from writing articles for
national media is that you hear from people who have
interesting stories to tell. I received a call from Peter
Gruchawka, a 70-year-old gentleman from Manorville,
New York, who reported that he had been diagnosed
with diabetes three months before and was put on 5
grams of an oral anti-diabetic agent. At the time, he had
a 5+ sugar spillover in his urine. He took the medication faithfully for about a month before he learned from
his wife who is a nurse that oral anti-diabetic agents can
damage the liver. Having read in *Herbal Medicine,* by
Diane Buchanan, and *Back to Eden*, by Jethro Kloss,
about the effectiveness of dandelions in controlling
diabetes, he decided to try them. Without saying anything to his doctors, he stopped taking the oral anti-
diabetic medication and began drinking dandelion coffee
each day. During the first week, his urinary sugar, mea-
sured night and morning, was erratic and unstable, but
after a week, his sugar stabilized and when he called, he
had been getting negative urine sugar readings for over
a month. The doctors are amazed and can't explain it.
An interesting side benefit to replacing oral hypoglycemic drugs with dandelion coffee is that, while oral anti-
diabetic drugs can damage the liver, dandelions are
known for strengthening the liver.

According to Mr. Gruchawka, he changed nothing but the medication. He had cut out pastries and other sugars when he was diagnosed and started on the oral hypoglycemic drug and has continued to do without those things while taking dandelion coffee.

In reporting all of these claims, however, I must add three qualifiers:

First, unfortunately, neither herbs nor synthetic remedies work for everyone in the same way. Different bodies respond differently to medicines, and what works incredibly well for one person may not work at all, or work less well, for someone else.

Second, good health results from a combination of healthy diet and enough exercise to keep the body toned. According to a mutual friend, Bob Stickle, for all his insistence that dandelions cured him, also changed his entire lifestyle. He didn't just add dandelion salad to what he was already doing.

Finally, and most importantly, people with health problems need to seek the advice and care of a competent physician with whom this information can be shared. It is important to reemphasize that it is presented as information only. I am not a medical doctor and neither advocate nor prescribe dandelions or dandelion products for any ailment. Only your doctor can do that (See Preface).

Because there are so many variables, it is hard to attribute cures to any one of them directly. For example, Italian farmers live a lifestyle which combines a healthy diet, lots of physical exercise in the form of work, and clean air. They heat and cook with wood, which they have to cut and split. They haul water for household use. When they move to the city, diet, exercise, and environmental conditions change. Stress and sedentary habits increase.

And there is always the element of faith in the healing process, whether it be faith in God or faith in the curative properties of the herb being taken.

While dandelions, given all these variables, may never be proven to cure any specific ill, they are an extremely healthy green vegetable which cannot in any way hurt anyone. Research on how much dandelions one would have to consume to cause harm indicates that eating grass is more dangerous than eating dandelions (Hobbs, 1985). Therefore, with everything going for dandelions, it is highly probable that everyone can derive at least *some* nutritional benefit by eating or drinking them regularly.

For medicinal purposes, dandelion is usually administered as a tea, tincture, or in powdered-capsule form. Formulas for these are contained in Hobbs (1985) and the *National Formulary*, as well as in practically all commonly-available herbals.

Dried dandelion leaf and root teas and tinctures are available in most health food stores as are dandelion root capsules. The capsules are packaged by several herb product manufacturers and are often combined with other herbs in blends designed for specific applications. For information about commercial sources, see Chapter 4.

One of the most convenient ways to get the benefits of dandelions is through an instant, roasted dandelion root beverage, **Thuna Instant Dandylion Blend**, which is caffeine-free, naturally sweetened by its own fructose, and inexpensive. See the order form at the back of this book for information. Recipes for making your own dandelion root coffee are contained in Chapter 8.

The medical and pharmacological establishment is generally critical of claims regarding the use of herbs against disease, and their concerns need to be put into perspective.

Herbal medicines have been used very effectively far longer than synthetics, and many current pharmaceutical products have been derived from research on plants used as medicine by many cultures. The problem with plants, however, is that they are available to anyone. It is impossible to patent a plant and gain proprietary rights to it. As a consequence, pharmaceutical companies attempt to isolate the active properties from medicinal plants and synthesize them so that they can patent the end product. Many of the synthetics have serious side-effects which were not present in the natural plant product, often because other chemicals in the plant compensated for them (*i.e.*, the large quantities of potassium in dandelions which allows for potassium replenishment when dandelion is used as a diuretic).

USDA botanist Dr. James Duke (1989) suggests that a proper and appropriate "herbal soup," filled with "vitamins, minerals, fibers and a whole host of bioactive compounds," from which the body can selectively strain the compounds it needs to restore itself to health, will be more effective than synthetic medicines containing a "very select and specialized compound or two plus filler, usually non-nutritive." This is especially true if the "herbal soup," in the form of a potent potherb like dandelion, is a regular part of the diet so that the appropriate bioactive substances are present in the right amounts when the body needs them.

Herbalist Cascade Anderson Geller, who teaches Medical Botany at the National College of Naturopathic Medicine in Portland, Oregon, says with regard to the increasing popularity of bitter greens, that "we're getting back to our ancestral tastes. It's a nice reminder that what we eat should be our medicine" (*Herbalgram* - Fall Winter 1988/89, page 9).

For a more detailed treatment of the historical, nutritional and pharmacological aspects of dandelions, you may obtain Christopher Hobb's complete *Monograph on Taraxacum Officinale* from the Eclectic Institute, 14385 S. E. Lusted Road, Sandy, Oregon 97055 (503) 668-4120.

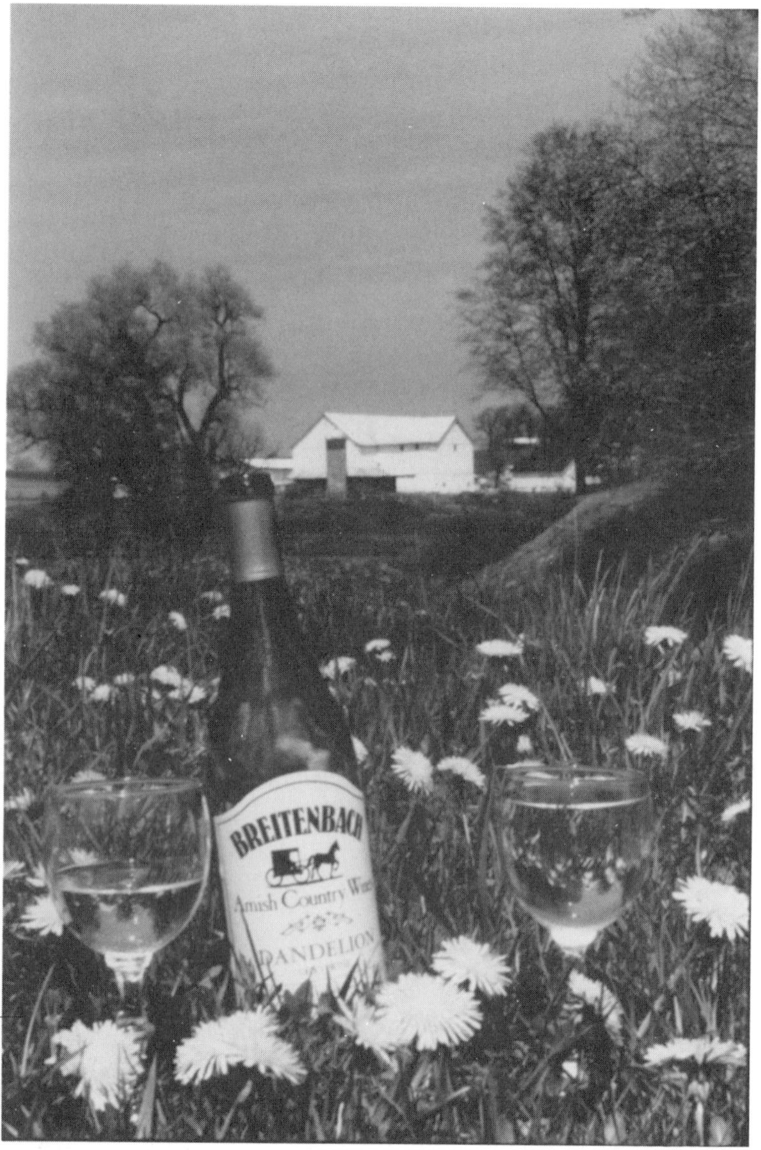
BREITENBACH
DANDELION

Chapter 4

Dollars in Dandelions

It's the ultimate irony that in the United States we spend millions on chemicals to eradicate one of nature's most beneficial vegetables, and then millions more on **lettuce**, which is so deficient in nutrients that, as Portia Meares, former President of the International Herb Growers and Marketers Association, says, it is nothing more than a "way California has of shipping water to the rest of the country!"

There are some enlightened souls, however. Americans each year spend somewhat over $3 million **buying** fresh dandelion greens at the market, and more millions on a large number of herbal preparations which range from capsules and tinctures to pet bird vitamins.

"Dandelion greens" (most of which are really blue-flowered chicory hybrids) are produced for the winter fresh market on farms around McAllen and Edinboro in Texas; near Orlando and Daytona Beach in Florida; in Sylmar, Fresno, and Oakland, California; and in Arizona. Those produced by Sam Scattaglia of L. and S. Dandelion and Sweet Anise Farm in Sylmar, California grow as tall as 2 1/2 to 3 feet! They grow them from seeds imported from Italy. Sam says, "Dandelions are the natural organic food. No crop-eating insects are interested in them, and therefore they are never sprayed with anything."

From February through October, Vineland, New Jersey, the nation's largest producer of fresh market dandelions and home of an Annual Dandelion Dinner (see page 79) is the primary supplier of true, wild-type dandelions. [1] Dandelion greens cultivated under protective plastic first appear on the market in February and last through April. From April through summer, Vineland grows the same hybrid varieties cultivated during the winter in Texas and Florida. A number of other small producers throughout the Northeast also enter the market in spring and summer, supplying local needs.

These greens are available in ethnic produce markets and supermarkets serving large ethnic populations in practically every major United States and Canadian city. The best way to find out who carries them in your area is to **call your local food terminal, ask which produce commission merchants handle dandelions, and call those commission merchants to see which retailers carry their dandelion greens.** In 1994 dandelion greens are selling for between $.69 and $.99 per pound.

If **canned dandelion greens** are more to your liking, W.S. Wells and Son, a small family-run farm and cannery in Wilton, Maine, have been canning them since 1886! They are sold under the "Belle of Maine" brand, and are available in three or six-can gift packs, complete

---

[1]   For information about Vineland, New Jersey, call or write the Vineland Chamber of Commerce, P. O. Box 489, Vineland, NJ 08360 (1-800-309-0019).

with a recipe booklet which contains recipes like the one for **Dandelion Spoon Bread** (see page 87). They also can fern fiddleheads. Adrian "Butch" Wells Sr., the third generation of the family canning dandelion greens, says, "Everybody tries like crazy to kill them, and we're shipping them to every state in the union as gourmet foods!" For information about their products, write W.S. Wells and Son, Wilton, Maine 04294.

If you wish to risk the wrath of your neighbors and **plant** dandelions in your garden, **seeds** for a number of dandelion hybrids are available through major and minor seed houses. These include:

- **Stokes Seeds, Box 548, Buffalo, New York 14240;**

- **Richter's, Goodwood, Ontario, Canada LOC 1AO;** and

- **Ferry-Morse Seed Company, Fulton, Kentucky 42041 and Mt. View, California 94042**

all of which sell the thick-leaved improved variety of the true dandelion, which matures in 95 days. Other seed houses handling dandelions are:

- **The Cook's Garden, P.O. Box 65, Londonderry, Vermont 05148**, which offers two French hybrid varieties;

- **Nichols Garden Nursery, 1190 North Pacific Highway, Albany, Oregon 97321**, which offers a cabbage leaved variety with a 95-day maturity; and

- **Abundant Life Seed Foundation, P.O. Box 772, Port Townsend, Washington 98368,** which sells wild dandelion seed in larger quantities (1 oz. to 20 lbs.).

"Italian Dandelion" seeds (the chicory varieties sold commercially as dandelions) are available from Botzum Seed Co., 43 E. Market St., Akron, Ohio 44308; Ferry-Morse and Johnny's Selected Seeds, Foss Hill Road, Albion, Maine 04910. They mostly will be listed as Catalogna, Italian dandelion, or just plain Ciccoria.

We have found seed companies to periodically be out of dandelion seeds, so you may have to try more than one.

You can also buy **roasted dandelion root coffee**, either as chunks of roasted root to steep in boiling water or in the form of an instant beverage much like "Pero" or instant coffee. Almost all dandelion root sold in the United States, raw or roasted, is imported from Germany, Belgium, or Eastern Europe. It is sold either granulated or "cut and sifted," which means that the roots had been cut into 1" sections before roasting and were screened to eliminate all small scraps before being packaged. The following companies sell dandelion leaves and roots on a wholesale basis. They can tell you who stocks their products in your area:

- **Frontier Cooperative Herbs, Box 299, Norway, Iowa 52318 (319) 227-7991;**

- **Whole Herb Company, 19800 Eighth Street, East, P.O. Box 1203, Sonoma, California 95476 (707) 935-1077;**

- **Blessed Herbs, 109 Barre Plains Road, Oakham, Massachusetts 01068 (508) 882-3839;**

- **Pacific Botanicals, 4350 Fish Hatchery Road, Grants Pass, Oregon 97527 (503) 479-7777.**

At least two **instant dandelion root beverages** are being manufactured in the world — the English **Symington's Dandelion Coffee Compound**, which, in 1984 was one of the top 100 best-selling herbal products at Holland and Barrett stores (Britain's equivalent to our General Nutrition stores) and **Thuna Instant Dandylion Blend**, which is produced in Canada. **Symington's**, which was developed in Edinburgh, Scotland in the 19th century by Thomas Symington to help alleviate his digestive problems, is not currently available in the United States, although about 35 tons of the product are sold each year in Great Britain and another 15 tons in Australia.

Thuna Dandylion Blend, which combines roasted dandelion root, barley, and rye in a caffeine-free, naturally sweet alternative to coffee with a remarkably similar flavor, is available in the United States through Goosefoot Acres, the exclusive importer. The price is $5.95 for an 80 gram (2.8 oz.) container, which makes from 70 to 100 cups of brew, depending on how strong you like it, for a cost of between $.06 and $.08 per cup. Until 1988, **Thuna's Dandylion Blend** had been available only in Canada, where about 6 tons (2,000-3,000 cases) are consumed annually. See the order form at the back of this book for more information.

For those suffering from PMS (see page 40), Traditional Medicinals, 4515 Ross Road, Sebastopol,

California 95472 (707) 823-8911 prepares **PMS Tea** in which the predominant ingredient is dandelion root. The tea is available in health food stores and wherever Traditional Medicinals products are sold.

Dandelion Flower Jelly is made commercially by several small local shops, including Orchard Ridge, 21170 S.R. 93, Logan, Ohio 43138 (614) 385-6230 and Coopers Mill, 1414 N. Sandusky Street, Bucyrus, Ohio 44820 (419) 562-4215. Recipes can also be found on page 108. **Dandelion wine** is produced by a number of wineries in the United States, including wineries in the Amana Colony in Iowa, and Breitenbach Winery, Rt. 1, C.R. 139, Dover, Ohio 44622 (216) 343-3603, which produces **Amish Country Dandelion Wine.** Jasper Carleton, a connoisseur of dandelion wine from West Virginia, told me at the National Wild Foods Association conference that the Breitenbach product ranked in the top 5% of all dandelion wines he had tasted! Breitenbach Winery will ship its wines anywhere in the United States. Ask to speak with Anita Davis if you call.

Many people, like Brassie Favretto (see page 78), sell dandelion sausage and other dandelion products locally from roadside stands.

Practically all respected herbal product companies manufacture formulations containing dandelion, including:

- **Turtle Island Herbs, Salina Star Rt., Gold Hill, Boulder, Colorado 80302 (303) 442-2215;**

- Planetary Formulas, P.O. Box 503, Soquel, California 95073 (408) 438-1700;

- HerbPharm, Williams, Oregon 97544 (503) 846-7464;

- Nature's Herbs, Inc., P.O. Box 336, Orem, Utah 84057 (801) 225-4443;

- Star West Botanicals, 11253 Trade Center Drive, Rancho Cordova, California 95742 (916) 638-8100 or (800) 880-4372;

- Nature's Way Products, P.O. Box 2233, Springville, Utah 84663 (801) 489-3631;

- Matol Botanical International Ltd. 870 Begin Street, Montreal, Quebec, Canada H4M 2N5 (514) 745-6300; and

- Eclectic Institute, 14385 S. E. Lusted Road, Sandy, Oregon 97055 (503) 668-4120.

The Eclectic Institute, Inc. which was started at the National College of Naturopathic Medicine in Portland, Oregon, is a pioneer in the freeze-drying of herbs. They market **freeze-dried dandelion root capsules**. Matol markets a product called **Km**, a liquid potassium supplement with 14 herbs including dandelion root. The others produce various formulations containing dandelion, including capsules.

The beauty of dandelions, however, is that you don't **have** to buy them, or their products! Dandelions are all around us, all year long, and they are **free**. So we might as well try them, right? There is no way they can hurt us and all kinds of ways that they can do us good, so we have everything to gain and nothing to lose!

All we have to know is when and how to collect them, and how to prepare them.

And that is what the rest of this book is about!

Chapter 5

Capturing And Dressing The Wild Lion's Tooth
Techniques for Collecting and Preparing Dandelions

The best way to rid your lawn of dandelions is to pick the leaves for greens, the blossoms for wine and jelly, and the roots for coffee. After a season or two of this, even dandelions get demoralized and disappear. After all, their whole reason for existing is to torment us, right? When they discover that we actually **want** them, what fun is left. So they disappear, and then you have to start scavenging your neighbors' lawns to satisfy the appetite you have developed for them!

The great blessing is that we don't have to spend a dime for the advantages of dandelions. However, for most people, their first experience with dandelions is also their last! They read in the paper, or a friend tells them, that dandelions are good. So they go out in mid-summer, grab some leaves from the lawn, make a salad or try them raw, and are put off by their extreme bitterness.

Maine humorist Tim Sample says that often it's what you leave out rather than what you say that makes Maine humor funny. Unfortunately, in the dandelion business, it's what folks have left out in telling how to collect and prepare the dandelion that has driven away many potential users, possibly you among them.

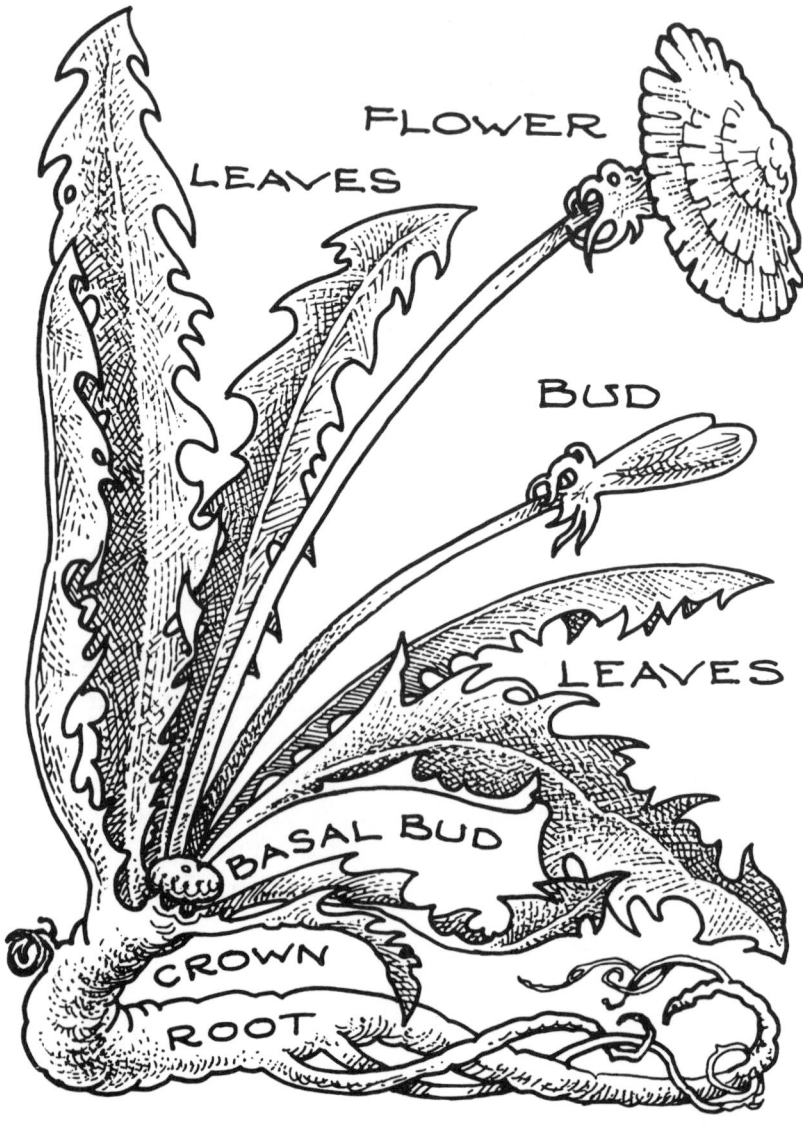

To insure that you have a good first experience with your dandelions, here is what you must do:

1. Collect dandelion leaves in the spring **before the flower buds appear. After that, they are too bitter to eat**, unless you follow the directions below. The best way to harvest is to cut the greens with the top of the root still attached so that the leaves stay together. This makes them easier to clean. A stirrup hoe, available from garden supply centers or hardware stores, is excellent for this task.

2. **Make sure that you collect the greens significantly back from the road and in areas which have not been sprayed with herbicide or pesticide.** Studies on heavy metal pollution conducted at Rutgers and Cornell Universities and by the National Research Council indicated that soil and plant lead concentrations, which generally are in the range of 15 to 25 parts per million parts of plant tissue (ppm), rose to 300 to 500 ppm near the edge of a heavily-traveled road. At 75 feet back from the road, or behind a building which blocked the pollutants, lead levels were those normally expected. In 1984, Kuleff, a radiochemist at the University of Sofia in Bulgaria, found that dandelion leaves accumulated heavy metals in amounts directly proportional to the presence of those metals in the surrounding environment, making dandelion leaves very effective monitors of air pollution (Hobbs, 1985). So be careful and collect only where the air and soil are relatively clean!

3. If **buds or flowers have already appeared** on your dandelions by the time you read this, there still is hope. **Wait until flowering is complete. Cut the old greens and flowers off at the root and let new greens grow. Harvest the new greens while young and tender and they will be only slightly more bitter than in early spring.** The best greens will be those which are allowed to grow in the rich soils of your vegetable garden. Ours grow on the perimeters of our raised beds and are delicious. We harvest our dandelions well into October each year and find them less bitter than store-bought greens.

4. To reduce bitterness even further, cover dandelions with a pot, slate, or some other device to blanch the greens as they grow. Blanching the greens will, however, reduce their nutritional properties.

5. Wash the greens thoroughly to get all the sand and grit out and peel off all old leaves.

If you would like your first experience to be with **cooked greens**, the basic method of cooking dandelion greens is as follows:

- Wash the greens thoroughly in slightly warm water, removing old, discolored, or badly broken leaves. Cut off the roots and any tough stems, and wash again, lifting the greens out of the water to allow any sand to settle in the pan. Then sprinkle the greens with salt.

- Cook the greens, with just the water which was clinging to the leaves after washing, in a tightly covered heavy pot or steamer until they are limp and barely tender, which takes between 5 and 10 minutes.

- Drain them and chop them fine.

- Dress the cooked greens with your choice of any of the items listed below.

The foods which complement and best reduce the apparent bitterness of dandelion greens are olive oil, garlic, pork or pork fat in some form, eggs, vinegar or lemon juice, cheese, and bread, plus a bit of salt and pepper. Combining one or more of these ingredients with raw or cooked dandelions is the best way to enhance your enjoyment of them. We particularly enjoy a sweet-and-sour dressing made by adding vinegar and brown sugar (or maple syrup) to hot bacon fat which we then pour over either raw or steamed dandelions just before serving.

If you prefer **raw greens**:

- Break the tender young leaves into a salad bowl.

- Add bacon bits (real or artificial), hard-boiled egg, your favorite cheese, tomato, and some garlic and/or onion. My wife rubs the bowl with garlic before adding the other ingredients.

- Dress the salad with either vinegar and oil or a sweet-and-sour dressing and top with garlic-flavored croutons.

This salad may be eaten alone or with bread — especially a piece of hard-crusted Italian bread. With sweet-and-sour dressing, we find the flavor reminiscent of a spinach salad with grapefruit sections added.

Seasonings used to flavor dandelions vary depending on who is doing the cooking. The French, Northern Italians, Swiss, Austrians, Germans, New Englanders, and Blacks in the Southern United States cook their greens with a chunk of salt pork, bacon, or ham, dress them with vinegar and often top them with hard boiled eggs. Greeks, Southern Italians, and Middle Easterners leave out the meat, dress the greens with olive oil, lemon or vinegar, garlic, and other herbs and spices (including hot peppers), and serve them with beans and pasta. Chris Hobbs, the author of the *Monograph on Taraxacum Officinale* (Eclectic Institute, Sandy, Oregon) says that **horta**, a stir-fry of chicory or dandelion greens, olive oil, thyme, sage, and other spices, which he enjoyed while in Greece, was one of the best-tasting dishes he has ever had. Other seasonings include sauteed onions, beets, chili sauce, and horseradish. The best suggestion is to experiment. Some say that after you have acquired a taste for dandelion's natural bitterness, you'll find there is nothing better than plain old buttered dandelion greens, seasoned with salt and pepper. If the bitterness still bothers you, however, you may further reduce it by letting the greens stand overnight in cold water or by cooking the greens in two changes of water with a bit of baking soda added to the first change.

Casseroles or salads with meat, beans and/or tomato, as well as dandelion quiches, mask bitterness. Serving dandelion greens on bread, for some reason which I cannot explain, completely eliminates the bitterness. I particularly enjoy fresh dandelion greens wrapped up in thin Greek or Middle Eastern bread, or loaded into the pocket of pita bread. Another of my favorite ways of eating dandelions is to make a **Dandelion Pizza Sandwich** out of bread, shrimp sauce (ketchup and horseradish), chopped raw dandelions and cheese. I prefer pita bread, English muffins or bagels and colby or cheddar cheese for this sandwich. Toast the bread. Spread shrimp sauce (or plain ketchup, pizza, or barbecue sauce if you prefer) over the surface. Add chopped raw or well-drained, cooked dandelions, top with thin slices of cheese, and microwave or broil until the cheese melts. Then eat and enjoy. I fed this sandwich to carpet layers and painters who were working on my house, and they raved about it. For a more elaborate pizza, see page 81.

This was your test. If the experience was a good one, dandelions are for you. If not, and you followed the rules, they still may be for you, but you have to add a couple of more steps to your processing to further mask the bitterness. As a last resort, you can look at it philosophically — anything that bitter **must** be good for you, right?

Many dandelion users collect enough greens in spring to last all year and freeze them. This is done by cleaning the greens, steam blanching them in a covered colander over a sauce pan for 1 1/2 to 2 minutes, and then plunging them into cold water to stop the cooking. The greens are then packaged in serving or recipe sizes in freezer bags and brought out as needed.

Another method of preserving dandelions, spinach, and swiss chard is by mixing the greens with 1/4 of their weight in dry salt and keeping them in a tight crock in a cool place. The salt may be removed from dry-salted vegetables by soaking them in fresh water (Firth, 1974).

Dandelion's diuretic property, mentioned in Chapters 2 and 3, is important enough to mention again. **If you are a heavy sleeper, don't eat or drink a lot of any dandelion product before going to bed.** One of dandelion's great medical values is as a spring tonic, which is another way to say that it is a **very effective diuretic.** It is used by many to do an internal spring cleaning — to flush out all the toxins which have been built up in the body over winter. If you are a relatively light sleeper and like to wake up early, this can work in your favor. Dandelions taken before retiring serve as an early morning wake-up call, like the Apache alarm clock of old. The earlier you want to get up, the more dandelions you eat or drink!

Chapter 6

Bacon, Vinegar, and Hardboiled Eggs
Recipes for Greens

The recipes included in this chapter are of two types — those which are prepared simply, with only garlic, some type of acid (vinegar or lemon juice), and vegetable oil and those rich in grains, eggs, meats and meat fat, cheese, and the other farm products which have always been available fresh to the farm families who created the recipes. Even though dandelions have been demonstrated to reduce cholesterol and to counter the heaviness of fatty foods, if you are concerned about cholesterol, gluten intolerance, and other dietary restrictions, you should find plenty of recipes in this collection which will meet your needs.

Keep in mind that many country cooks don't measure ingredients but add "a little of this and a little of that" until the dish they are preparing "tastes right." Ingredients are added in rough proportion to one another, with no exact quantities, and in many such recipes the quantities of ingredients have been estimated. Feel free to adjust ingredients to your own taste preferences. If a particular recipe which intrigues you falls short of your expectations the first time you make it, experiment with it until it tastes right to you.

When using dandelions, be aware that one pound of fresh dandelions yields 2 quarts of fresh greens, or 1 1/2 to 2 cups of cooked greens. In recipes which call for canned dandelions, one pound of fresh greens, cooked until tender, can be substituted for one 15 oz. can of dandelions.

I generally prepare dandelions in one of the variations presented in Chapter 5 or in an omelet.

Dandelion Omelet

3	strips bacon
4	eggs
4	mushrooms (sliced)
1	cup or so of fresh dandelion greens, chopped fine
1/2	cup (total) grated mozzarella, provolone, muenster, or similar white cheese and/or grated colby longhorn or mild cheddar cheese

For the filling: fry the bacon crisp in an omelet pan. Remove from pan and crumble into a small bowl, reserving the fat. Sautee the mushrooms in the remaining bacon fat (which can be reduced by half if you wish). After the mushrooms have sauteed for a minute or so, add the dandelions and sautee until wilted. Remove the mushrooms and greens to the same bowl containing the bacon and set aside.

The quick and easy omelet is made by scrambling the eggs lightly, adding the cheese and dandelion filling, and cooking until the eggs reach the desired firmness. Makes 2 servings.

When I have time and want a true gourmet treat, I pour a portion of the eggs into a very hot frying pan greased with butter or bacon fat. I stir the top layer of eggs lightly, being careful not to disturb the layer in contact with the frying pan. When the eggs are almost cooked, I add part of the bacon, vegetable, and cheese filling, fold the omelet in half and continue cooking until the cheese melts, serve it, and then make a second omelet. The recipe above serves two.

We often eat the quick and easy version between two slices of bread or heaped on a buttered English muffin, and I tell you, if they ain't got these in heaven, I ain't goin'!

Another very simple way to consume dandelion greens is raw between two slices of any kind of buttered bread, or in place of lettuce in a meat or cheese sandwich. A dash of vinegar, Worcestershire, or Tabasco sauce makes it even better.

Rural Italians have perfected the art of preparing their beloved "ciccoria" (pronounced "chigōda") better than anyone, except maybe the country folks from the south of France who consider it a gourmet treat.

Italian recipes vary in character and ingredients from region to region, but all are highly creative and extremely nutritious.

Most meals start with salad. One of the best Italian salads is served by Robert Fatica, maitre'd of **Primo Vino** in Cleveland, Ohio's "Little Italy." Fatica claims that "on a Friday evening, even though we have an excellent salad bar, one out of every three people orders dandelion salad." He makes each salad to order. The following recipe provides amounts, but consider these only as guidelines.

Fatica's Dandelion Salad

4	cups fresh dandelion greens
1/3	cup garbanzo beans or chick peas
1/4	cup shredded sharp cheese such as fontinella or fontina
1/3	cup each of julienned mozzarella, ham, and salami
1/4	cup thinly sliced red onion
1	sliced tomato
3	Tbsp. olive oil
2	Tbsp. wine vinegar
	salt, freshly ground black pepper, garlic, oregano, basil, dried parsley
	fresh grated Romano cheese

Mix the ingredients (except Romano cheese) in a large salad bowl, season to taste with salt, pepper, garlic, oregano, basil and dried parsley, and toss thoroughly. Lay all ingredients on a platter, sprinkle grated Romano cheese on top, and serve with Italian bread. One of Fatica's secrets is to add a little of each seasoning, toss it to mix it thoroughly, then add some more, until the flavor is the way he wants it.

Dandelions and beans, whether fava beans, kidney beans, or lentils, are a staple in many Italian diets. Olga Carl, from Naples, Italy, prepares **Dandelion with Kidney Beans (Ciccoria Fagioli)** the following way:

1	lb. dry kidney beans
5	qts. water
2	cloves of garlic, crushed
1/4	cup olive oil
8	oz. (1/2 can) stewed tomatoes, cut fine
3 - 4	lbs. fresh dandelion greens
1/2	tsp. black pepper
	salt to taste

Put 3 qts. water in a large (6-10 qt.) soup pot and boil. Add beans. Brown garlic in oil, then add the oil and garlic mix to the cooking beans and cook until tender. Add tomatoes and continue cooking.

In a separate pot, boil 2 qts. water. Wash dandelion greens thoroughly and chop or tear into pieces of reasonable size. In enough water to cover the greens, cook until tender (about 15-20 minutes). Drain well, but save the dandelion liquor to add to tomato juice or drink straight — it's loaded with vitamins! Toss the dandelions into the pot of beans, season with pepper and salt, and stir frequently with a wooden spoon for 5-7 minutes. Serve with Italian or garlic bread. Makes 6-8 servings. Any leftovers can be frozen in quart containers and reheated later in the microwave. This same dish, made with 1 1/2 cups pasta instead of dandelions, is called "Pasta Fagioli", and the two can be combined — both dandelions **and** pasta can be added to the beans.

This recipe can also be made with canned beans.

The dandelion liquor saved from the above recipe is probably the healthiest part of the dish. It can be made into a delightful **Dandelion Juice Cocktail** as follows:

28 oz. juice from boiled dandelion
4 oz. tomato juice
2 tsp. freshly-squeezed lemon juice
1 Tbsp. Worchestershire sauce
salt and pepper to taste

Mix the ingredients and serve chilled. This makes one quart and serves four or more depending on the glass size.

The cocktail can be converted into a **Dandelion Gelatin**:

4 oz. unflavored gelatin
green food coloring
pineapple chunks (drained) or canned fruit cocktail (drained)
chopped walnuts
whipped cream (optional)

Heat one quart of **Dandelion Juice Cocktail** (see above recipe) and add unflavored gelatin. Bring it to a boil; mix in food coloring, small wedges of pineapple or fruit cocktail, and/or chopped walnuts. Pour into glass dishes or a jello mold, chill until firm, and serve with a dollop of whipped cream or mayonnaise and a maraschino cherry.

Olga's **Dandelion Salad**, which goes with the above, is made from fresh-washed, drained greens, to which a little pepper, a little salt, some olive oil, vinegar, and garlic powder are added.

According to Sammy Scattaglia, who grows dandelions for market in Sylmar, California, Italian farmers live to the age of 90-95 years on a diet made up predominantly of "ciccoria and beans"!

The Scattaglia's are from Adelphia, Mondrone, (Bari), Italy. Pina Scattaglia's favorite recipes are for **fried dandelions, steamed dandelion with garlic and chili, plain old boiled dandelion greens, and dandelion with spaghetti.** She also adds boiled greens to chicken soup, lima beans, lentils, and fava beans. Her salad is the same as Olga Carl's (above) but with quartered tomatoes added.

Fried Dandelion

	dandelion greens
2 - 3	eggs
	flour
	garlic salt
	chopped mint

Boil the dandelion greens for 10 minutes and drain well. Make a batter with the eggs, flour, garlic salt, and chopped mint which is thick enough to stick to the greens.

Heat any light vegetable oil in a frying pan. Dip each piece of dandelion in batter. Fry one side and then the other. After frying, sprinkle with Romano or Parmesan cheese on top. Serve hot.

Steamed Dandelion with Garlic and Chili Peppers

4 - 5	qts. fresh dandelion greens
1	cup water
1/2	cup extra virgin olive oil
	garlic, salt, pepper, chili pepper flakes

Clean and finely chop the dandelion greens. Put a **maximum** of 1 cup water in the bottom of a 6-quart saucepan, insert a steamer rack, and place the dandelion greens on top. Cover the greens with 1/2 cup of 100% pure extra virgin olive oil, 1 — 2 cloves of garlic, salt, pepper, and chili pepper flakes. Cover and steam until tender. Serve. **Tip:** you don't want too much water, because you don't want it to mix with the oil.

Boiled Greens

Prepare dandelions as for **Steamed Dandelions with Garlic and Chili Peppers** (see above) but boil them in water until tender instead of steaming and do not add the spices. Drain and save pot liquor for drinking and to reheat the dandelions. Garnish greens with a bit of olive oil and lemon and serve. The cooking water is filled with vitamins and minerals and can be made into Dandelion Juice Cocktail (see page 68).

Dandelion with Spaghetti

First Variation

1	lb. (or more) fresh dandelion greens
1/2	lb. uncooked spaghetti
3	cloves garlic, minced
1	16 oz. can stewed tomatoes
1/4	cup light vegetable or olive oil
	grated Romano or Parmesan cheese
	hot pepper flakes

Boil fresh greens in a large pot of salted water until almost tender. Add spaghetti to pot and cook until spaghetti is done.

In a large skillet, sautee garlic in oil until lightly colored. Do not let the garlic burn. Add tomatoes. Simmer 10 to 15 minutes and put tomato sauce on top of drained spaghetti and dandelions. Top with hot pepper flakes and cheese.

Second Variation

Clean and chop dandelion greens and boil in water to cover until tender. Add raw spaghetti to boiling dandelions and cook together until spaghetti is done.

Lightly sautee minced garlic in oil. Lift the cooked dandelion and spaghetti mixture from the water, keeping plenty of water with it, and combine with the oil and garlic. Mix together, heat, and serve.

The use of garlic, olive oil, and lemon juice is a clear indication that a recipe originated in either southern Italy or Greece!

Mary Zone, a prominent Cleveland, Ohio political figure of Italian descent, prepares a delicious dandelion quiche, which is one of the best quiches of any kind I have ever tasted. Here is her recipe:

Dandelion Quiche

3 1/2	cups fresh dandelion greens
1/2	lb. mushrooms
9	eggs
1/2	cup grated Romano cheese
	9" unbaked pie shell
	oil, garlic, and cloves
	fresh parsley
	pepper

Partially bake pie shell in 450° oven for 5-7 minutes or until lightly browned. Remove from oven and reduce heat to 325°. Set shell aside.

Cook dandelion greens in salted, boiling water until well wilted but not completely cooked (about 2 minutes). Drain thoroughly in colander or squeeze all liquid from greens. Cut greens into small pieces. Sautee garlic, greens, and mushrooms in oil until all liquid has evaporated.

Beat eggs in a bowl. Season to taste with fresh parsley, cheese, and pepper.

Put greens into the baked pie shell. Pour egg mixture over greens and bake at 325° until eggs set and a knife blade inserted just off center comes out clean, about 40 minutes. Let set 10 minutes before serving. As an option, the greens and egg mixture may be placed directly into the pie or quiche pan without any pie shell.

We use a quiche recipe which doesn't require so many eggs that we have adapted from a *Better Homes and Gardens* article on Lambsquarters (another wild vegetable which resembles spinach) (page 196-7, May 1977). The quiche tastes similar but is lower in cholesterol and cost.

1	9" unbaked pastry shell
1	Tbsp. all-purpose flour
1 3/4	cups milk
3	eggs
2	cups shredded natural Swiss cheese
4	cups fresh dandelion greens
	light vegetable or olive oil
2	cloves minced garlic
1/2	lb. sliced mushrooms
1/2	tsp. salt

Partially bake the pastry shell in a 450° oven for 5 to 7 minutes or just until it is lightly browned. Remove from oven; reduce heat to 325°. Set the shell aside.

Prepare the vegetables as in **Dandelion Quiche** (see recipe above). After the water has evaporated, stir in the flour.

In a mixing bowl, beat together the eggs and milk, and add the cooked vegetables. Sprinkle the cheese in the partially-baked crust and pour the egg and vegetable mixture over it. Bake in a 325° oven for 40-45 minutes or until a knife blade inserted just off center comes out clean. Let it stand 10 minutes and serve. Makes 6 servings.

And then there's Bert Greene's **Crustless Greens Pie**, which he describes as follows.

> For centuries, greens were more beloved by peasants than by princes. With good reason too, for the populace most often used what was closest at hand for their dinner table. One such devise is a great personal favorite. I found it in Eze, but I suspect its genesis is closer to the Italian border. It is a crustless pie made up of all the greens, onions, peppers, and zucchini a farm wife can carry from a garden in her apron. No cousin to either quiche or pizza, it could substitute admirably for each without a second thought. And more to the point, perhaps, it is the quintessential one-dish vegetarian meal.

1 1/2	lbs. Swiss chard
1/2	lb. arugula
3/4	lb. dandelion greens
3	Tbsp. unsalted butter
1	Tbsp. olive oil
1	onion, finely chopped
2	cloves garlic, minced
1/2	small yellow pepper, seeded and finely chopped

2	small zucchini, grated
1/3	cup chopped fresh basil
1/4	cup chopped fresh parsley
1/2	tsp. salt
1/4	tsp. freshly ground black pepper
3	extra large eggs, lightly beaten
1/4	cup freshly grated Parmesan cheese
1/4	cup grated Jarlsberg cheese
1/4	cup fresh bread crumbs

Trim the chard, arugula, and dandelion greens. Discard the stems and chop the leaves. Preheat the oven to 375°. Heat 1 Tbsp. of the butter with the oil in a medium saucepan. Add the onion and cook one minute. Add the garlic and cook one minute longer. Stir in the pepper, chard, arugula, dandelions, zucchini, basil, parsley, salt, and pepper. Cook covered, over medium heat, until very tender, about 15 minutes. Remove the cover and cook, stirring frequently, until all liquid has evaporated, about 25 minutes. Transfer to a large mixing bowl.

Beat the eggs into the greens and pour the mixture into a buttered 9-inch glass or ceramic quiche pan. Sprinkle with the Parmesan and Jarlsberg cheeses.

Melt the remaining 2 Tbsp. butter in a small skillet over medium heat. Stir in the bread crumbs and sautee until golden. Spoon them over the pie. Bake 25 minutes. Let stand at least 10 minutes before serving. Serves six (Greene, 1984).

Dandelion Soup is another Italian specialty, and Mary Zone's is one of the finest! Here is how she makes it:

12	cups (3 qts.) sparerib stock (from parboiled spareribs)
2	onions
6	carrots (and any leftover vegetables in refrigerator)
	fresh parsley
1	head cabbage
4	cups parboiled dandelions
1	lb. Italian sausage (hot or mild according to taste)
1/2	lb. ground beef
4	slices bread
	garlic salt, pepper, parsley
	grated Romano or Parmesan cheese

Prepare sparerib stock by parboiling spareribs, then setting the liquid in the refrigerator overnight. Skim off the grease the next day. Into 12 cups of sparerib stock, add the onions, carrots, parsley, cabbage (which counters the bitterness of the dandelion), dandelion greens, and the sausage, chopped thinly. Bring to a boil and cook over medium heat for 45 minutes.

While the above is cooking, mix ground beef with 4 slices of crumbled bread, and season with garlic salt, pepper, parsley, and cheese. Form into tiny balls.

After the vegetables and sausage have cooked 45 minutes, add the tiny meatballs and all leftover, precooked vegetables; cook for 15 minutes longer, or until the meatballs are done. Let stand 10 minutes before serving.

Italians also make a wonderful lasagna with dandelions. This recipe came from *Prevention Magazine*, April, 1982.

Dandelion Lasagna

2	qts. water
2	lbs. dandelion leaves
2	cloves garlic, minced
3	Tbsp. chopped parsley
1	tsp. oregano
1	Tbsp. basil
1/2	cup wheat germ
3	cups tomato sauce
6	oz. tomato paste
9	whole wheat lasagna noodles
1	tsp. olive oil
1	lb. Ricotta cheese
dash	Cayenne pepper
1/2	cup grated Parmesan cheese
1/2	lb. mozzarella cheese sliced thinly

Bring water to a boil, add dandelions, and cook until tender. Remove dandelions with a slotted spoon and reserve the cooking water. Place dandelions in a blender with garlic, 1 Tbsp. parsley, basil and oregano. Blend thoroughly, but be careful not to liquify the greens. Add wheat germ, two cups tomato sauce, and tomato paste. Blend just enough to mix thoroughly and set aside.

Bring reserved cooking water back to a boil. Add lasagna noodles and olive oil. Cook until just tender but still firm (about 5-8 minutes), drain, and reserve. Mix ricotta cheese, cayenne, and the remaining 2 Tbsp. parsley; reserve.

Lightly butter the bottom of a 9" x 13" baking pan. Position three lasagna noodles side by side as a first layer. Cover with 1/3 of the dandelion sauce, then 1/2 of the ricotta cheese. Shake some Parmesan cheese over the ricotta and cover with a layer of mozzarella slices. Repeat.

Layer the final three lasagna noodles and the last 1/3 of the dandelion sauce. Cover with the remaining Parmesan and mozzarella cheese and one cup tomato sauce. Bake at 375° for 30 minutes. Makes 10-12 servings.

Vineland, New Jersey is the "Dandelion Capital of the World," at least when it comes to growing and selling the wild type, yellow-flowered dandelions. Brassie Favretto, who has been growing and eating dandelion greens for over 50 years, invited me for lunch one day and served the best **Italian Sausage** I had ever eaten. Naturally, it was made with dandelions! Here is his recipe. If you decide not to make 100 pounds at a time, you'll have to cut it down to size.

100	lbs. ground pork or meat mixture of your choice
2+	lbs. salt, depending on taste
10	oz. finely ground pepper
2	whole bulbs garlic

1   qt. inexpensive red wine
20-25   lbs. dandelions, chopped coarsely

Break garlic bulbs into cloves, peel, and crush them through a garlic press into the wine. Let stand overnight. The next morning, mix together all ingredients well and stuff into sausage casings.

You may want to adjust the garlic, salt, and pepper to suit your taste. The way Brassie made it suited mine just fine.

Vineland has for many years held an annual Dandelion Dinner, a creation of its former mayor, Pat Fiorilli, who was the best publicist for dandelions "what ever was!" until his passing in 1989. As a publicity gimmick for the 1987 dinner, Patrick planned dandelion soup **with real lion meat**, but ran afoul of health authorities who claimed he had no import permit for the lion meat! So he had to substitute beef for the real lion meat, which he and his dog, Bozo, consumed afterwards.

Pat Fiorilli's Dandelion Soup

2   qts. dandelion greens
2   qts. chicken stock, homemade, bought, or skimmed
1/2   cup rice or 1 lb. egg noodles (both optional)
1   lb. mixed ground beef, veal, and pork (or real lion meat if you can pull it off!)
1   egg
2   Tbsp. bread crumbs
2   Tbsp. minced parsley
1   Tbsp. minced onions (extra fine)

1/4	tsp. salt
1/8	tsp. seasoned pepper
dash	nutmeg
3	Tbsp. grated Parmesan cheese
2	Tbsp. sour cream (optional)

Bring chicken stock to a boil. Add dandelions. Cook gently. Add rice or noodles, if desired. Make very tiny meatballs out of the remaining ingredients, except the nutmeg, cheese, and sour cream. When the greens are tender, add meatballs and cook gently for 10 minutes or until the meatballs are thoroughly cooked. Serve hot, garnished with nutmeg, cheese, and sour cream (Fiorilli, 1981).

The Italians also make bread out of dandelions and other greens. This recipe comes from Jean Presti of Presti's Bakery in Cleveland, Ohio's Little Italy neighborhood:

Dandelion Bread

1	lb. dandelion greens
	salted water to cover dandelions
2	cloves fresh garlic, minced
1/4	cup olive oil or other light vegetable oil
	pepper
	grated mozzarella or Parmesan cheese
1	qt. lukewarm water
3 - 4	lbs. flour

1 oz. salt
2 oz. cake yeast

Boil dandelion greens until tender and drain **well.** Chop. Add garlic, oil, and black pepper to taste. Add grated cheese and mix in well.

Make bread dough by combining water, flour, salt and yeast. Roll out thinly. Spread dandelion mixture over the dough and roll the dough into a loaf. Brush the top with garlic oil and cut slits across the top. Raise for 20 minutes. Bake at 350° until golden brown, about 15 — 20 minutes.

The original recipe makes a delicious loaf, but it can be varied by adding cooked, crumbled Italian sausage and/or sauteed mushrooms.

These last two Italian recipes were contributed by Christine Juliano Casey of Mayfield Village, Ohio:

Dandelion Pizza

prepared pizza dough
olive oil
4 cups finely chopped dandelions
1 clove garlic, minced
2 Tbsp. Parmesan cheese
juice of 1/2 lemon
shredded mozzarella cheese

Prepare pizza dough using whatever recipe you prefer, and let rise. When ready to bake, place in 350° oven on a cookie sheet and bake until golden, but not brown, about 10-12 minutes. Remove from oven and brush on olive oil with a pastry brush. Let cool slightly.

Steam dandelions and drain well. Brown garlic in olive oil and add greens to it. Mix in Parmesan cheese and lemon juice. Spread greens on top of the baked crust and top with shredded mozzarella cheese. Return to oven for about 10 minutes or until cheese melts.

Dandelions with Cornmeal

4	cups fresh dandelion greens
4	Tbsp. olive oil
2	cloves garlic, minced
	Parmesan cheese
1	cup corn meal
1	cup cold water
1 1/2	cups boiling water
1/2	tsp. salt
	shredded mozzarella cheese (optional)

Steam greens until tender. Heat 2 Tbsp. olive oil, add garlic, and allow to brown. Add the tender dandelions to the olive oil and garlic. Sprinkle with Parmesan cheese and toss.

Mix corn meal and cold water. Add boiling water and salt and cook, covered, over hot water (about 10-15 minutes).

In a 10" skillet, warm the remaining olive oil, then add corn meal and pat it into the pan. Place into an 350° oven for 20 minutes. Turn cornmeal over and bake 20 more minutes. Remove from skillet when brown and crusty. Place in serving dish, top with dandelions, cut into pie shape, and serve. If desired, shredded mozzarella may be sprinkled on top of the dandelion and melted in the oven before serving.

The Amish and Mennonites, along with others of Pennsylvania German and Dutch extraction, have some very imaginative and tasty recipes for dandelion greens. Some of our favorites include:

Hilda Naftzger's Traditional Pennsylvania German Recipe for Dandelion Gravy

Hilda is the lady I referred to on page 23. Here is her recipe:

1/2	lb. ham, diced into small pieces
3 - 4	cups buttermilk
2	eggs, beaten
2	Tbsp. flour
1	lb. fresh dandelion greens
	boiled potatoes

Brown diced ham in an 8" to 10" skillet and add buttermilk. Beat eggs with flour, thinned with a small amount of buttermilk to eliminate lumpiness. Add eggs and flour to the skillet and bring to a boil. Put washed, chopped dandelions into the skillet. Let the mixture return to a boil and boil for 2 minutes. Serve over potatoes. (Variation on Amish dandelion gravy recipe).

The Amish make several variations of dandelion gravy. The one we like best is a **Sweet and Sour Dandelion Gravy** which is made as follows:

2 - 3   strips bacon, diced
1   Tbsp. flour
1   cup cold water
2   Tbsp. sugar
      salt to taste
2   Tbsp. white or cider vinegar
2   hard-boiled eggs, diced
1   cup finely chopped fresh dandelion greens
      sour cream or buttermilk (optional)

Fry the bacon in a pan and preserve the drippings. Use part of the drippings to make pan gravy with flour. When brown, stir in water and let boil. Add sugar, salt, and vinegar to taste. A bit of sour cream, or buttermilk may be added. Fold in diced eggs. Add the dandelions just before serving ("Aunt Becky", 1977).

This mixture can be served alone as a side dish or over potatoes, rice, or pasta.

Sue Byler, a Conservative Mennonite from Middlefield, Ohio, makes another variation.

1/2-1   lb. bacon
3-4   Tbsp. bacon drippings
4   Tbsp. flour
      milk
      fresh dandelion greens
4-6   hard-boiled eggs, sliced
      cooked potatoes, rice, or noodles

Fry bacon and set it aside. Pour off all but about 3-4 Tbsp. of bacon fat. Add flour, stir till smooth, and then brown in the skillet. When brown, add milk slowly until the consistency of gravy is the way you want it.

Blanch cut-up dandelion greens by pouring boiling water over a colander full and let greens drain thoroughly. Add greens, eggs, and 8-12 slices of crumbled bacon to the gravy mixture. Serve over cooked potatoes, rice, or noodles.

You might like to experiment with all three to see which one you like best.

Dorothy Nichols Hibler, whose German and Dutch ancestors founded Logantown, Pennsylvania, shared a recipe handed down to her by her mother and grandmother for **Dandelions with Egg and Bacon Sauce**. No exact quantities are given; add the ingredients in rough proportion to one another:

1 - 2	lbs. fresh dandelion greens
3 - 6	eggs, depending on the amount of dandelions
1	lemon for every two eggs
1/2-1	lb. bacon

Tear dandelions into small pieces and boil or steam until tender. Drain well and set aside, but save the pot liquor to drink separately for its vitamins.

Cut bacon (amount depends on the amount of dandelion greens) into small cubes and fry in a large skillet until crisp. Drain off all the fat except what is needed to cook the eggs.

Break 3-6 eggs into a bowl, add the juice of 1 lemon for every 2 eggs and mix thoroughly. Pour the egg and lemon mix over the crumbled bacon in the skillet and cook only until it reaches a sauce-like consistency. Pour this mixture over the drained dandelions, mix thoroughly, and serve.

The original recipe called for vinegar instead of lemon juice and for far less bacon. In fact, Dorothy says, "sometimes it seemed that Mother just passed a piece of bacon through it! In fact, Mother didn't stir the sauce in, she just poured it over the top. If some of the children got too greedy with the sauce and didn't take enough dandelion, Mother would tap them on their knuckles with her fingers. When I grew up, I decided to embellish it with more bacon and with lemon instead of vinegar to make the dish more elegant!" Dorothy's modifications show how recipes evolve over time in the hands of creative people.

No sampler of dandelion recipes would be complete without a good Maine "downeast" recipe or two. Beatrice Comas shared the traditional **Downeast Way of Making Spring Greens**:

"If you have what we in Maine call a large "fondness of greens," you will need:

1   lb. salt pork (with lean layers to add flavor)
1   qt. water
1   lb. fresh dandelion greens
     peeled potatoes
     paprika

Dice the pork in thick pieces, score them, and put them in a large kettle with the water. Cover and bring to the boiling point. Lower the heat and cook the pork for about 1 hour.

About 1 1/2 hours before you plan to serve the greens, wash them thoroughly, drain, and place them in the pot with the pork and water. Cover and bring to a boil, stirring occasionally so that the flavor of the pork will permeate the greens. Let them cook for 1 hour, making sure that they do not stick to the pan.

Now place potatoes well down into the greens. Cover the kettle and bring back to the steaming point. Lower the heat and cook until potatoes are tender, about 1/2 hour. When greens are done, heap them on a preheated platter and surround with the boiled potatoes which will have taken on a slightly green tinge. Dot with paprika if desired. Lay the strips of salt pork atop the greens and now you have an old-fashioned Maine dandelion green dinner (Comas, 1979).

Likewise, there has to be at least one recipe from Adrian (Butch) Wells, owner of the company which has been canning **"Belle of Maine" Brand Dandelion Greens** since 1886! This is our favorite:

Dandelion Spoon Bread

1   pkg. frozen onions in cream sauce
1   15 oz. can dandelions, drained (see page 48) or equivalent (see page 64)
1   cup dairy sour cream
2   eggs, slightly beaten

1/2   tsp. salt
1   8 1/2 oz. pkg. corn muffin mix
1/2   cup melted butter or margarine
    shredded Swiss cheese

Cook onions in cream sauce according to package directions. In large mixing bowl, combine onions in cream sauce, dandelions, eggs, sour cream, butter or margarine, and salt. Stir in corn muffin mix. Pour mixture into greased 1 1/2 quart casserole dish. Bake in 350° oven for 30-35 minutes or until wooden pick inserted in center comes out clean. Sprinkle top of corn bread with shredded Swiss cheese. Bake about 2 minutes more or until cheese is melted. Serve spoon bread warm. Makes 8 servings (Wells & Son, n.d.).

And if your tastes tend toward Southern fare, Dr. Tom Squier, a naturopath and wilderness survival instructor for the U.S. Army, contributed the following two recipes for dandelion greens. These recipes appeared in his "Living Off the Land" column in the Moore County, South Carolina *Citizen News Record* (April 12, 1989)

Dandelions and Grits Baked Casserole

2   cups chopped cooked dandelion greens
1   cup uncooked grits
2   eggs beaten
2   cups diced ham chunks
1/2   cup grated Parmesan cheese
4   cups water
1/3   tsp. salt

8   oz. shredded cheese, cheddar, swiss or blend
1   Tbsp. mustard

Add grits to boiling, salted water in a large saucepan and stir to prevent sticking. Cover, reduce heat, and simmer five minutes. Add well-drained dandelion greens, swiss or cheddar cheese, and ham chunks. Stir until cheese melts. Fold in eggs and mustard and pour into greased baking dish. Sprinkle the grated Parmesan cheese on top and bake at 325° for 45 to 50 minutes or until toothpick inserted in center comes out clean.

Layered Dandelion Green Salad

1   quart chopped dandelions
1/2 cup chopped green pepper
1/2 cup chopped celery
1/2 cup plain yogurt
1/2 cup mayonnaise
1   cup shredded cheddar cheese
2   cups sprouts, bean or alfalfa
1/4 cup chopped wild onion (with tops included)
2   cups tender green pea pods or tender redbud tree pods
2   Tbsp. honey
1   cup bacon crumbles

Drain the well-washed dandelion leaves and tear into pieces. Greens must be well-drained to prevent sogginess. Put a layer in the salad bowl. Add a layer of onion, celery, pepper, pea pods, and sprouts. Sprinkle with cheese and bacon. Drizzle with combined yogurt, honey, and mayonnaise. Repeat these three layers until you run out of ingredients. Refrigerate overnight to allow cooling and the flavors to mix.

For those interested in an authentic French recipe for the famous **"Pissenlit au lard"** (or "Salade de Pissenlit") to share at your next gourmet feast, here is one:

Salade de Pissenlit Menagere
(Dandelion Salad Country Style)

1	lb. fresh dandelion leaves
2	Tbsp. pork fat
1/2	cup very small diced bacon, salt pork, or diced fat
1	Tbsp. vinegar
	salt and freshly ground pepper to taste
1	Tbsp. fine herbs (parsley, chives, tarragon and chervil)

Clean dandelion leaves and cut into small pieces. Melt pork fat in a saucepan and add very small diced fat, salt pork, or bacon; sautee until brown. Dry greens and sprinkle with pork and cooking fat. Add vinegar, a little salt, pepper, and chopped fine herbs. Toss and serve immediately (Diat, "Menu Classique" in *Gourmet*, XIV, No. 3, March, 1954, pp. 24-56).

In the Provencal region of Southern France, another delightful salad, called **Mesclun**, is served. Mesclun originally was made of a mixture of tiny wild spring greens that were collected by the local folk and brought to market in sacks. Seeds for the ingredients for Mesclun can be purchased from **The Cook's Garden**, a seed house in Londonderry, Vermont (See page 49).

Mesclun (Provencal Mixed Salad)

```
1       slice dry white bread
1       clove garlic
3 1/2   Tbsp. olive oil
1       Tbsp. white wine vinegar
        salt and ground black pepper
```
Each of as many of the following as are available: lambs lettuce, rocket (arugula), chervil, dandelion leaves, endive, cress, and lettuce.

Dry bread for 20-30 minutes in a preheated oven. Rub each side with a garlic clove. Pile salad greens loosely in a bowl large enough to toss the combined ingredients. Combine oil and vinegar and season to taste with salt and pepper. Pour over salad, toss well, and mix in the bread, broken into croutons. Serve immediately (Boxer et. al., n.d.).

Artist Henri de Toulouse Lautrec was also a famous gourmet. He particularly favored dandelions and liked them as follows:

```
        fresh dandelion greens
        olive oil
        salt, to taste
        wine vinegar
        pepper
        prepared mustard
3 - 4   hard-boiled eggs, mashed
```

1   clove garlic
     bread

Wash greens and dry with a cloth. Dress dandelions with olive oil, salt, wine vinegar, pepper, and a small spoonful of mustard. Add eggs and blend thoroughly. Serve on bread rubbed with garlic (Dunn, 1977).

The Slovenians have an excellent recipe for creamed dandelion which was shared with me by a student:

Creamed Dandelion, Slovenian Style

1 - 2   lbs. fresh dandelion greens
5   strips bacon
2   Tbsp. onion, minced
1   heaping Tbsp. flour
2   Tbsp. sugar
1   egg, beaten
1/3   cup vinegar
2   Tbsp. water
         salt
2   hard-boiled eggs

Wash the dandelion greens and boil them in a covered pot in salt water until tender. Drain. Chop bacon and fry with 2 Tbsp. minced onion. In a bowl mix all remaining ingredients well and pour over browned bacon and onion. Stir constantly. Cook until thickened. Pour over greens and mix well. Garnish with sliced hard boiled eggs (Michelle Gaultier).

Following is a recipe for Southern style greens which we particularly like. It is similar to the dandelion greens dish described in Chapter 3 which was enjoyed by Al Brown of the Buffalo Bills. This recipe, or one nearly identical to it, graces the tables in many Black and Southern Appalachian white households.

Mixed Greens, Southern Style

1	bunch each mustard, chicory, and dandelion greens (collard and/or turnip greens may be substituted for chicory)
1/2	lb. bacon or ham
1 - 2	red pepper pods
1	Tbsp. cider vinegar
	chopped scallions or onions
	salt and freshly ground pepper

Wash greens well and cut off any tough stems. Put into a colander and pour boiling water over them. Drain and place them into a pot with the meat and pepper pods and pour fresh boiling water over them to barely cover. Cover the pot. Simmer about 30 minutes, then add vinegar, salt, and pepper to taste. Remove the cover so that the cooking liquid can reduce somewhat and simmer 15 more minutes. Drain, reserving liquid.

Place greens in the middle of a platter and arrange the meat around it. Garnish with chopped scallions or onions. Serve with homemade cornbread and cups of the pot liquor to dip the cornbread into (Silverman, 1977).

Another way to make this dish is to sautee the ham or bacon and chop it into small pieces, chop the greens into small pieces, and mix them all together in the cooking pot. Greens and meat are then served together from a bowl.

Hazel Pruitt, of the Cuyahoga County Cooperative Extension Service, prepares a dynamite version of greens which she serves each year at the Urban Gardeners Recognition Dinner in Cleveland, Ohio. When I asked for the recipe, she said she uses no recipe, just goes by feel. When pressed, however, she gave the ingredients and rough proportions as follows, with the counsel that whoever makes them should adjust the quantities to their taste.

9   lbs. finely chopped dandelion, turnip, mustard, and/or collard greens

2   Tbsp. vegetable seasoning or equivalent in mixture of black pepper, salt, red pepper, seasoned salt and/or other greens seasoning

1   lb. smoked pork butt or other smoked meat including smoked turkey (the smoked meat gives the mixture flavor)

Put all ingredients in a pan with about 1/4 inch water in the bottom and cook 2 hours or until the greens turn from light to dark and lose their raw taste. By that time, the meat should have fallen off the bones. Remove bones, finely chop meat and mix it throughout the greens.

A couple of other recipes we are particularly fond of are:

Dandelion Casserole

1	lb. ground beef
1	can (16 oz.) whole tomatoes
1	clove garlic, minced
1	Tbsp. parsley, chopped
1/2	tsp. oregano
1/2	tsp. basil
	salt and pepper to taste
2	cups fresh dandelion greens, cleaned

Brown the beef and drain. Add tomatoes and seasonings. Simmer for a few minutes and place in a casserole dish and bake at 350° for 30 minutes. Meanwhile, boil the dandelions, drain, and chop them into small pieces. After casserole has baked for 30 minutes, add the chopped dandelions and stir. Return casserole to oven for an additional 15 minutes.

Foraged Asparagus and Dandelion — Oriental Style

1/2	lb. asparagus (wild if possible), washed and sliced on the diagonal
1	Tbsp. butter or margarine
1 1/2	cups young dandelion leaves and buds
1	Tbsp. vegetable cooking oil
1 1/2	Tbsp. soy sauce
1	tsp. corn starch
1	cup chicken or beef broth
	pepper to taste

Sautee asparagus, dandelion leaves, and flower buds together in butter and oil in a skillet. When asparagus is tender but still crisp, turn off the heat. Combine soy sauce and corn starch and blend until smooth. Add chicken broth, pour into skillet of vegetables, and cook, stirring constantly, until sauce thickens. Add pepper to taste and serve at once. Serves four.

The small white section of the dandelion which connects roots and leaves is called the "crown." (See diagram on page 56). It, too, is good eating. It lacks the bitterness of the leaves and tastes a bit like artichoke and asparagus combined. When you clean your dandelions, save the crowns in a separate bowl and prepare according to one of the recipes below to serve as a separate side dish.

Basic Dandelion Crowns

fresh dandelion crowns (about 6 per person)
salt to taste
butter or margarine
fresh ground pepper

Put washed dandelion crowns into a pot with water just to cover. Bring to a boil, simmer for 5 minutes, strain, and repeat, this time adding a dash of salt to the water. Strain, return to the pot with a pat of butter and a dash of freshly ground pepper. Heat slowly until butter melts and serve (Good, n.d.).

Marinated Dandelion Crowns

	fresh dandelion crowns (about 6 per person)
1/2	cup olive oil
1/4	cup vinegar
1	tsp. salt

1/4   tsp. ground pepper
1   clove garlic, sliced
1   small onion, finely chopped

Prepare dandelion crowns as in the above recipe (Basic Dandelion Crowns) but don't add butter. Drain crowns thoroughly. In a ceramic or glass bowl, mix olive oil, vinegar, salt, pepper, garlic, and onion. Add the crowns and marinate at least four hours before serving.

Dandelion beer is very popular with workers in iron foundries and potteries in the West Midlands and around Stoke-on-Trent, England. Many bring a quart of dandelion beer to work every day because it is, according to Phillips (1986) "refreshing and particularly good for relieving stomach upsets and indigestion and for clearing kidneys and bladder."

Dandelion Beer is made as follows:

1/2   lb. young dandelion plants, washed with hairy
       side roots removed from the tap root
1   gallon water
1   lemon
1/2   ginger root, peeled and crushed
1   lb. light brown sugar (demerata)
1   oz. cream of tartar
1   Tbsp. dried yeast
4   tsp. light brown sugar for bottling

Place well washed dandelions, ginger root, and water in a large pan with the thinly-pared rind of the lemon, making sure the white pith is removed. Bring the mixture to a boil and boil for 10 minutes. Put the sugar and the cream of tartar into a large container. Strain in the liquid from the dandelions. Stir until the sugar dissolves and cool the mixture to body temperature. Add the lemon juice and sprinkle the yeast over the top. Cover and leave in a warm place to ferment for three days or until fermentation stops. Strain off any sediment and bottle the liquid, adding 1/2 tsp. brown sugar per pint. Leave the beer undisturbed until it clears (about one week) (Duff, 1982; Phillips, 1986). According to Phillips, the beer is ready to drink when "it hisses as the stopper is loosened. It does not keep very long. Test the bottles daily to see that they don't get too fizzy. Even after only 2 days in the bottle it is smashing."

This might be a good brew for house painters working on old homes to try to protect themselves against the effects of ingesting lead.

For those of you wishing to serve something exotic to your friends at those special spring parties, this next section of recipes, which focuses on dandelion hors d'oeuvres and gourmet dishes, is for you.

Dandelion Spread
(Crostini di girasoli)

This is a Northern Italian specialty, designed to be served with toasted rounds of bread or on crackers.

1/2	lb. dandelion, watercress, or spinach leaves
10	oz. cream cheese at room temperature
2	oz. anchovy paste or 3 anchovy fillets, chopped fine
1/4	tsp. white pepper

Remove roots and tough stems from dandelions; wash and drain well. Place dandelions, cream cheese, anchovies, and pepper in container of an electric blender or food processor and process until smooth. Transfer to a serving bowl and use as a spread. Makes about 1 1/2 cups (Candler, 1980).

Dandelion Dip

1/2	cup young dandelion leaves, chopped finely
1/2	cup cottage cheese
1/2	tsp. salt
	dash of pepper
1	tsp. chopped chives or onion
	sesame seeds

Put dandelion leaves, cottage cheese, salt, pepper, and chopped chives or onion into blender or food processor and blend mixture thoroughly. Chill before serving. Garnish with sesame seeds and serve with crackers or celery (Good, n.d.).

For those of you looking for something really special to serve at that exquisite party you are throwing, here are three recipes:

Pate of Leafy Greens

4	cups spinach
1	cup dandelion or chicory greens
2	cups watercress
3	medium yellow onions, finely chopped
1	Tbsp. finely chopped garlic
1/4	cup butter

1	Tbsp. chopped basil leaves
1	tsp. fresh chopped thyme leaves
4	slices dry white bread or baguette with crusts removed
6	oz. ground sausage
1/2	tsp. salt
4	large eggs

Preheat oven to 350°. Wash and de-stem the greens. Steam over boiling water in a basket until limp, about 2 minutes. Squeeze out the water with a wooden spoon while the greens are still in the basket. Chop the greens.

Sautee the onions and garlic in butter over medium heat until the onions are translucent. Mix with the greens. Add the herbs and spices.

Soak the bread in the milk for fifteen minutes. Squeeze the milk out with your hands. Cut the bread into small pieces. Mix with the greens. Crumble the sausage and cook until it loses its pink color. Drain off any oil and add the sausage to the greens.

Beat the eggs with a wire whisk and pour into the greens/sausage mixture. Mix until well blended.

Butter the sides of a heavy mold 3 inches deep and 6 inches in diameter. Pour in the mixture and bake for 1-1/4 hours. Cool on a wire rack for thirty minutes. Refrigerate for two hours. Run a knife around the edge of the mold. Place in a bowl of just boiled water for thirty seconds. Turn upside down over a serving plate lined with greens and tap gently. You can make this pate the day before you plan to serve it. Accompanied with a little creme fraiche or freshly made ricotta, it would make a wonderful summer lunch (Brennan, Glenn, and Cronin, 1985).

Greens-Stuffed Pork Chops

1	lb. Swiss chard OR
3/4	lb. collard, turnip, or dandelion greens
4	Tbsp. (1/2 stick) unsalted butter
1	clove garlic, minced
1	small onion, finely chopped
1/4	cup heavy or whipping cream
2	Tbsp. red wine vinegar
1 1/4	cups stale bread cubes
	salt and freshly ground black pepper
4	double pork chops with pockets for stuffing
1	cup dry white wine
2	Tbsp. cornstarch
	chopped fresh parsley
2	tsp. water

Trim the chard or other greens and discard the stems. Chop the leaves. You should have about 1 cup.

Preheat the oven to 350°. Melt 3 Tbsp. of the butter in a medium saucepan over medium heat. Add the onion and cook one minute. Add the garlic; cook two minutes. Stir in the chard or other greens and cook, covered, tossing occasionally, over medium-low heat until tender, about fifteen minutes. Remove the cover and stir in the cream and vinegar. Cook until thickened, about five minutes. Stir in the bread cubes and salt and pepper to taste. Mix well. Remove from the heat.

Stuff the pork chop pockets with the greens mixture. Close the pockets with wooden toothpicks.

Melt the remaining 1 Tbsp. butter in a Dutch oven over medium heat. Sautee the pork chops until well browned on both sides. Pour the wine over the chops. Bake, covered, turning once, for one hour.

Remove the chops to a platter and keep warm. Mix the cornstarch with the water in a small bowl until smooth. Stir the cornstarch into the cooking juices. Heat to boiling and reduce the heat. Cook until slightly thickened. Spoon over the pork chops. Sprinkle with parsley. Serves four (Greene, 1984).

And a couple of whimsical dishes which should delight your family and friends:

Green Drink Surprise

1   cup spinach, parsley, mint, dandelion tops and/or beet greens
2   cups pineapple juice
15   drops liquid artificial sweetener

Blend a few of these greens in 2 cups pineapple juice for every 1 cup fresh greens. Add sweetener. Drink (Manning, n.d.).

Dandelion Green Noodles

This recipe is the creation of Millie Owen who relates this story about her discovery.

This started as a whimsical experience when I weeded a plot of dandelions and wanted to do something with them. I substituted them for spinach in our usual recipe for green noodles, and the dandelions made the noodles both tastier and a brighter, darker green. The basic recipe also works for other greens — lambsquarters, kale, swiss chard, and of course spinach. Just adjust the amount of flour to the moisture in the greens until you have a stiff dough. Cook homemade noodles by boiling for about 8 minutes and serve them as you would the ones you buy. These are so flavorful that they are simply good just tossed with butter and grated cheese. The recipe makes about one pound.

4 oz. (about 2 packed cups) finely chopped dandelion greens
2 eggs
1 tsp. salt
1+ cups flour

Put dandelion greens and eggs in blender, blend till smooth. Place in bowl, add salt, and start beating in flour. Continue until dough is very stiff. Turn dough out onto a floured surface and knead about five minutes. Roll dough with a floured rolling pin until it is a noodle-thin sheet. Let stand to dry for about one hour, then cut it into strips of whatever width you like. It is best to use fresh noodles the day you make them. You can refrigerate for a few days between layers of paper towels (Owen, 1984).

And, finally, to top it all off, one of several desserts made from dandelion leaves:

Dandelion Meringue Pie

Crust:

2/3	cup whole wheat flour
2/3	cup rice flour
3	Tbsp. butter or margarine
3	Tbsp. vegetable oil
2	Tbsp. ice water

Filling:

4	egg yolks
2/3	cup honey
2	Tbsp. whole wheat flour
1 1/2	cups milk
1	cup cooked, chopped dandelion leaves, squeezed dry
1/2	cup pine nuts or sunflower seeds
2	tsp. grated orange peel

Meringue:

4	egg whites
2	Tbsp. honey

To make crust, combine pastry and rice flours in a small bowl. Cut in butter or margarine with two knives or a pastry blender. Add oil and mix until dough looks crumbly. Stir in ice water, a little at a time, using only enough to hold dough together. Mix until you can gather the dough into a ball. Press the dough into a lightly greased 9" pan.

To make filling, combine egg yolks with honey and flour in a saucepan. Gradually beat in milk. Cook over a very low heat, stirring constantly until thickened. Do not let it scorch. If lumps form, pour the custard through a strainer. Puree the dandelion in a blender or food processor. Add to the custard and stir in pine nuts and orange peel. Pour into pie crust and bake at 350° for 20 minutes.

In a clean bowl with clean beaters, beat egg whites until stiff. Gradually add honey. Be careful to add the honey *very slowly* or else the whites will fall. Remove pie from oven and mound the meringue over it, spreading all the way to the crust. Return the pie to the oven for an additional 10-15 minutes until meringue is golden. Serves 6-8 (*Prevention Magazine*, April, 1982).

This barely scratches the surface of recipes for greens and crowns. If you try all these and want more, write us and we'll see what we can do!

Chapter 7

The Art of Peeling Dandelions
Cooking with the Lowly Dandelion Flower

It's spring. You look out on a sea of yellow blossoms which should be green lawn. You have three choices. You can spend your day eliminating them. You can do nothing and watch your lawn become a dandelion ranch! Or you can do what caused the British to finally form a "Save the Dandelions Society," because their dandelions were disappearing so fast! You can convert those blossoms to tasty tidbits and magnificent morsels! But first, you must learn the art of peeling dandelions!

There is an art to peeling dandelion flowers, make no mistake about that! One can't just rush in blindly, tossing flowers here and there. It simply doesn't get the job done. Say, for example, you need 1 quart of peeled flowers for the Amish dandelion jelly recipe. No problem, right? Wrong! The first time we tried it, we felt that only the Amish, maybe a few Italian Catholics, and Mormons have within their families a large enough labor force to accumulate that many peeled dandelion flowers without spending all day at it!

Peeling dandelions can be a lot of work, especially if the recipe requires that you completely remove the green parts, which are quite bitter (see diagram on page 56). If the flowers are tightly closed, with the yellow sticking far enough above the green to allow a firm grip on the flower — as is the case early in the morning — the job is much easier to do. Grasp the flower firmly with one hand, then pinch the flower hard at the bottom, where the yellow attaches to the green, shake a bit, and the yellow falls out. It's still a lot of work, however. It was with great relief that I learned, on talking to the Amish lady who submitted the recipe below, that she just clipped the stem off flush with the base and boiled the flower, green and all.

I was introduced to **Dandelion Flower Jelly** in the home of an Amish friend some years ago. She got the recipe from the "Cooking with Maudie" column in the national edition of *The Budget*, an Amish-Mennonite newspaper published in Sugarcreek, Ohio. This is the recipe.

Dandelion Flower Jelly

1	qt. dandelion blossoms (without stems)
1	qt. water
1	pkg. Sure-Jell®
1	tsp. lemon or orange extract
4 1/2	cups sugar

In the early morning, pick blossoms. Remove and discard the stems. Wash the flowers well and then boil the blossoms in the water for 3 minutes. Drain off 3 cups of the liquid and discard the blossoms. Add Sure-Jell®, lemon or orange extract, and sugar. Boil for 3 minutes, then skim off the foam on top. Put in jars and seal. Its taste resembles honey and is good on any bread (Miller, 1983).

Our experience so far has been that this recipe produces a jelly with a thin consistency. Reducing the liquid to 2 2/3 cups firms it up nicely.

Since discovering the above recipe, I found another version in an article by Marilyn Kluger, which is similar except that she used 5 1/2 cups of sugar and 2 Tbsp. lemon juice. With 5 1/2 cups of sugar, 3 cups of liquid would probably be just right, but we prefer reducing the dandelion liquid and using less sugar for a slightly less sweet jelly. Try both and decide which you like best. I also find the lemon extract (or juice, depending on the recipe you use) to be more complementary to the dandelion flavor than the orange extract, but this is just a personal preference.

If you would like something on which to spread that dandelion jelly, you might try these tasty muffins, the recipe for which was found in Chris Nyerges' book, *Wild Greens and Salads*.

Dandelion Flower Muffins

2	cups unbleached flour
2	tsp. baking powder
1/2	tsp. salt
1/2	cup dandelion flowers
1/4	cup vegetable oil
4	Tbsp. honey
1	egg, beaten
1 1/2	cup milk

Combine all dry ingredients. In a separate bowl, mix together the liquid ingredients and then add the liquid to the dry ingredients and stir just to moisten. The batter should be lumpy. Spoon into an oiled 12-cup muffin tin and bake in a preheated oven (400°) for 20-25 minutes (Nyerges, 1979).

Another taste treat which will amaze your friends and make you the talk of the neighborhood is dandelion flower cookies, which a gourmet friend of mine, known for his prowess in the kitchen, tasted and pronounced "healthy!"

Dandelion Flower Cookies

1/2	cup vegetable oil
1/2	cup honey
2	eggs
1	tsp. vanilla extract
1	cup unbleached flour
1	cup dry oatmeal
1/2	cup dandelion flowers

Blend the oil and honey and beat in the 2 eggs and vanilla. Stir in the flour, oatmeal, and dandelion flowers. Drop the batter by teaspoonfuls onto a lightly oiled cookie sheet. Bake in a preheated 375° oven for 10-15 minutes (McPherson, 1979).

Another way to convert dandelion flowers to something sweet and tasty is to make **Dandelion Syrup**

6	oz. dandelion flowers
2/3	pint water

6   oz. sugar

Pour the boiling water into the dandelion flowers and leave standing for 24 hours. Strain and add the sugar. Bring to a boil and boil gently until the consistency of syrup is reached. Bottle and sterilize. This recipe makes about 1 1/4 cups (O'Ceirin, 1978).

Ruth Kahl of Charlotte, North Carolina, who now, with the passing of Pat Fiorilli of Vineland, New Jersey, stands alone as the most enthusiastic and innovative dandelion promoter I have ever met, has invented a dandelion syrup that she calls **Amber Nectar**. Kahl uses the syrup in myriad recipes.

2   cups boiling water
2   cups dandelion blossoms (with as much green removed as possible)
1 1/2   cup sugar
1/8   tsp. salt

Pour the boiling water over the dandelion blossoms, stir, and allow mixture to cool for a couple of hours. Swish the blossoms around in the jar and set in the refrigerator for eight hours (or overnight). (Note: Stirring once yields a delicate flavor and light color. Stirring/swishing blossoms around in the jar now and again while cooling yields a stronger flavor and darker color.) Strain. Add sugar and salt to the liquid and stir. Bring the mixture to a full boil and continue for 5 minutes at a rolling boil. Serve with French toast, pancakes, etc.

She freezes the blossoms from which the nectar is drained (which she calls "Lion Paws") in ice cube trays, and incorporates them in a whole bunch of other recipes, including **Cream of Weed** soup:

3/4	cup Lions Paws
4	cups milk and/or stock
3/4	tsp. salt
1/4	tsp. paprika
2	Tbsp. butter or margarine
1	Tbsp. grated onion or 1 tsp. wild onions or wild garlic run through a press
2	Tbsp. flour
dash	paprika
	grated Parmesan cheese
	sliced hard-boiled eggs
	crumbled bacon slices
	croutons

Combine the lions paws, milk (or stock), salt and 1/4 tsp. paprika in a blender and puree. Heat the puree in a saucepan. In a separate pan sautee the grated onion in the butter or margarine, and stir in flour. Combine with the puree and simmer for five minutes. Garnish with one or more of the remaining ingredients on the list.

To make croutons, cube whole wheat bread slices. Sautee wild onion or garlic (domestic will do) and other herbs, such as Carolina Bay and finely chopped basil, in unsalted or salted butter until the onion is transparent. Add the bread cubes. Brown.

Dandelion flowers have also been mixed with eggs in breakfast omelets, batter-fried as appetizers, and sauteed as side dishes. Recipes which we have enjoyed include this one.

Dandy Omelet

1   cup dandelion flowers
4   eggs
2   Tbsp. butter or margarine
     salt and pepper to taste

Pick dandelion buds which are showing yellow about halfway down the bud. Remove stems, wash, and measure one cupful. Melt butter in a medium-size omelet pan. Add the drained and dried dandelion buds and sautee just until the buds start to burst open. Pour in lightly beaten eggs. As eggs firm up along the edge, lift around the edge with a spatula to let liquid egg run under, cooking until the omelet is firm all around but still soft in the center. Fold into thirds. Flip over, continue cooking until done, and serve. Season to taste with salt and pepper or sprinkle some finely chopped dandelion leaves over the omelet for garnish. Serves 2-3 (Hanle, 1971).

DiPalma's (1981) version of this omelet calls for two cups of younger, unopened buds, fried in butter until they pop. Then add the eggs, salt and pepper, and cook until done. This is not as fancy, but still tasty. DiPalma also has a recipe for opened flowers, which are mixed with the eggs in a blender:

Dandelion Yellow Flower Omelet

2   cups open flower buds
2   Tbsp. butter or margarine
4   eggs
     salt and pepper to taste

Wash the opened buds thoroughly and place in a blender with the eggs. Add salt and pepper and blend thoroughly. Add butter to the skillet and pour in egg and flower mixture. Cook until done (DiPalma, 1981).

Organic Annie Miller's *Wild Food Delights* is the source of **Golden Dandelion Blossom Waffles**, a delightful recipe which has the double blessing of containing no flour, making it ideal for gluten-intolerant folks.

Golden Dandelion Blossom Waffles

2	cups whole millet
1/2	cup hulled sunflower seeds
5	cups water

Soak the above ingredients overnight in a large bowl. In the morning, drain through a mesh sieve, discarding the soaking water. Rinse under running water.

2	cups water
1	cup packed dandelion blossoms
1	tsp. vanilla extract
1	tsp. nutmeg
1	egg or 1 tsp. guar gum (a binder for non-gluten containing grains)
2	tsp. baking powder

Combine the above, half at a time, with the soaked grain mixture and blend to a smooth batter. Pour or ladle onto a greased waffle iron; reduce liquid to make pancakes.

If you are searching for some special appetizers for your spring party and have an abundance of dandelion flowers at your disposal, you might like to try one or more of the following:

Mock Mushrooms (Morels)

Dandelion flowers can be deep-fried in batter to make delicious snacks or hors d'oeuvres that taste a little like morels prepared the same way. The blossoms are pollen-rich, making them nutritious as well as tasty.

1	qt. (or a colander full) fresh dandelion blossoms
4	qts. water salted with 2 Tbsp. salt
1	cup cracker crumbs
2	Tbsp. milk
1	egg
1/4	tsp. salt
1/8	tsp. pepper
1/2	tsp. parsley
1	Tbsp. Parmesan cheese

Pick new dandelion blossoms — those on short stems — and soak them in the salted water for 3-4 hrs. Rinse and drain well. Cut off the stem ends close to the flower heads, leaving only enough to hold the petals together (the stems and greenery are bitter).

Make the batter by combining the milk, egg, salt, pepper, parsley, and Parmesan cheese.

Roll the dandelion flowers in cracker crumbs and then dip into egg batter. Dip again in cracker crumbs. Drop the batter-coated blossoms into deep hot fat (375°)

and fry until lightly browned or fry in hot butter till brown. Drain on absorbent paper, sprinkle with more salt, if needed, and serve at once as a hot hors d'oeuvre or over rice or scrambled eggs.

If you like your hors d'oeuvres sweet, this version may be more to your liking:

Fried Dandelion Blossoms With Honey

	fully opened dandelion blossoms
1	cup milk
1	egg, beaten
1	cup flour
1/2	tsp. baking powder
1/2	tsp. salt
	honey to taste

Choose only fully opened blooms, being sure to remove all of the bitter stem. Next, thoroughly combine the milk, egg, flour, baking powder, salt, and honey in a bowl. Dip the blooms into batter and drop into hot oil over a medium heat. Fry until golden brown. Remove and drain on absorbent paper. Serve hot or cold.

For fancy parties, there is Haley's version:

Dandelion Fritters

36	dandelion blossoms
1	cup ice water
1/2	tsp. salt
1	egg, beaten

1   cup unbleached, all-purpose flour
     oil for deep frying

Rinse the dandelion blossoms in cool water and drain thoroughly. Snip off as much of the stem and greenery as possible while leaving the blossom intact.

Preheat the oil for deep frying. Prepare the batter just before frying. Stir the ice water, flour, and salt together. Beat in the egg. The ice water helps create a crisp lacy effect when the blossoms are fried. Dip the blossoms in batter and deep fry until golden. Drain on paper towels and serve immediately (Haley, 1986).

And finally, the ultimate appetizer:

Pickled Dandelion Buds

1   quart young dandelion flower buds, still tightly
     closed
1   tsp. salt
1   clove garlic, crushed
1   cup white vinegar
1/4 cup brown sugar
1   cup water
2   Tbsp. dill seed
     pinch of cloves

Remove the stems from the dandelion buds and cover them with water. Boil for 5 minutes. Pack the buds in a sterilized canning jar or jars. In a saucepan, combine the vinegar, sugar, water, salt, dill seed, garlic, and cloves. Boil for 10 minutes and pour over the dandelion buds. Seal tightly and store for one month before using (Crowhurst, 1973).

Dandelion flowers may also be made into a delightful soup.

Dandelion Petal Soup

2	Tbsp. butter
2	Tbsp. onion, finely chopped
2	Tbsp. flour
4	cups milk
1	tsp. salt
1/4	tsp. pepper
	pinch of nutmeg
2 1/2	cups dandelion petals

Melt the butter in a heavy saucepan. Add the onion and sautee until tender. Add the flour and blend well. Scald 3 cups of the milk and add gradually to the flour mixture, stirring constantly. Add the salt, pepper, and nutmeg. Simmer for 20 minutes. Add 2 cups of dandelion petals and stir. If soup is at all lumpy, beat a little. Add the remaining milk gradually, stirring. Simmer for another 10 minutes. Garnish with the remaining 1/2 cup of dandelion petals (Hanle, 1971).

The most commonly known use for dandelion flowers, however, is in the making of dandelion wine. What most people don't know, though, is that dandelion flowers can also be used to make a couple of non-alcoholic or only semi-alcoholic beverages.

Teetotaler's Dandelion Beverage

1	qt. fresh dandelion blossoms
2	qts. boiling water
3	cups sugar
2	cups cold water
2	lemons, sliced thin
2	oranges, sliced thin

Fill a quart measure firmly with fresh dandelion blossoms. Rinse and cut off the stem very close to the flower heads. Cover with boiling water and set aside to cool. Combine the sugar with the cold water and bring to a boil; this will make 3 cups of syrup. Add the syrup, oranges, and lemons and let the mixture stand for 2-3 days. Strain and serve over cracked ice. To keep longer, either bottle the strained liquid and cork tightly or keep under refrigeration. Makes more than 2 quarts of a healthful non-intoxicating drink (Kluger, 1984).

If you don't mind something mildly alcoholic, you might want to try Dandelion Fizz:

Dandelion Fizz

5	cups prepared dandelion flowers
8	cups (1/2 gallon) water
2	lemons
4	cups sugar

Trim the stalks from the flowers but leave the green sepals on and discard any overblown flowers or unopened buds. The prepared dandelions should fill a 1 quart measure when gently pressed down. Wash the flowers in a colander and tip them into an earthenware, enamel, or plastic container with a well fitting lid. Pour the boiling water onto the dandelions, cover the vessel with a lid, heavy board, or weighted plate, and leave to stand for 12 hours. Strain the liquid through a double thickness of muslin into a large saucepan. Add the sugar and the pared rind and juice of the lemons. Heat gently and stir until the sugar has dissolved but do not allow to boil. Strain the liquid into jugs and leave to cool. Pour into clean, dry bottles with strong screw caps. The brew is ready to drink in 3 to 4 weeks. The drink is very mildly alcoholic and, although sweet, is quenching, with a hint of the lightest lager flavor. Serve in tall glasses half filled with ice and garnished with a sprig of mint or lemon balm (Michael, 1980).

If your pleasure is more strongly alcoholic, and you don't want to wait a long time for the brew to age, this Dandelion Cordial may be for you:

Dandelion Cordial

2-3	cups dandelion flowers
2/3	cup sugar
	rind of 1/2 lemon
1	qt. vodka

Use unwashed dandelion flowers with the green parts removed. Mix all the ingredients together and pour into a jar. Cap tightly and put away in a dark place. Shake every day to make sure the sugar dissolves. Let stand two weeks, then strain through filter paper. Store in a bottle with a tight-fitting cap.

This cordial is not syrupy-sweet. It has a pleasant, unusual flavor and a fine, dark yellow color. It is nice by itself or on ice with a slice of lemon. As a toddy with hot water and honey, it is soothing for colds and coughs or just pleasant and warming on a cold winter night. Makes approximately one quart (Silverman, 1977).

And finally, for the dandelion wine aficionado, we offer the following variations on the common theme, from which you can choose, as it were, your own poison. Be aware, however, that those who partake of this potent stuff report no noticeable effects while drinking, but watch out the next morning! Maude Grieve, in *A Modern Herbal* (1937), says of dandelion wine, "This wine is suggestive of sherry, slightly flat, and has the deserved reputation of being an excellent tonic, extremely good for the blood."

Dandelion Wine (Old Recipe)

3	qts. dandelion flowers
2	lemons
1	orange
3	lbs. white sugar
1	pkg. (1/4 oz.) active dry yeast
1	slice toast

Remove the green parts of the dandelion flowers and place the flowers in a large, clean crock or jar. Bring 4 qts. of water to a boil and pour it over the flowers. Let stand three days, stirring once a day. On the fourth day, pour the contents of the crock into an enamel kettle. Squeeze the lemons and orange and set the juice aside. Add the sugar and lemon and orange rinds to the flowers and water. Bring all ingredients to a full boil and simmer for one hour. Add the citrus juices, let cool, and pour it all back into the jar. Soften the yeast in 1/4 cup of warm water, spread this paste on a slice of toast, and float it on top of the liquid. Let it stand for 3 to 6 more days. Now strain the liquid, pour it back into the jar, and let stand overnight. Next day, strain through filter paper and pour into clean sterilized bottles. Cork lightly until the bubbling (fermentation) stops (about 3 weeks) and then secure the tops firmly and store. Let the wine mature at least six months before drinking. Makes approx. 3 qts. (Silverman, 1977).

Haley's (1986) version varies only in using 2 oranges and in adding 1 lb. of raisins with the citrus juices. A Polish recipe contributed by Gary Budzinski uses 4 qts. of dandelion flowers, 3 oranges and 3 lemons, diced.

If you are the impatient type and want to get the job done quickly, you might want to try Bracket and Lash's technique, which uses the same ingredients but speeds up the process considerably. As with the above recipe, you can use either one or two oranges, and add raisins if you desire:

Dandelion Wine

3	qts. dandelion blossoms (yellow, fully open and dry)
4	qts. boiling water
3	lbs. sugar
1	orange
2	lemons
1	cake yeast

Collect the dandelions as early in the day as possible because the mixture must cool to 100° and that takes some time. Pour the boiling water over the blossoms. Let the mixture stand 3 hours; do not stir. Strain the mixture into a big cooking pot and add the sugar, orange and lemon rinds. Cook over medium heat for 15 minutes. Cut up the orange and lemons and place them in a 2 gallon crock or plastic pail. Pour the cooked mixture on top of the fruit. When the mixture cools to 100° (a little warmer than body temperature), add the yeast which has been dissolved in 1 cup of the warm mixture. Let it stand 12 hours and strain once again. Return the mixture to the crock, cover and let it stand 2 months. Strain into bottles and sample it in 6 months (Brackett & Lash, 1975).

Another quick recipe, but one which gets the brew to your tummy faster, was contributed by Dorde Woodruff of Salt Lake City. She got it from her landlady's daughter in Evanston, Illinois, and names it after her:

Mari's Dandelion Wine

4	qts. dandelion blossoms
4	qts. boiling water
6	oranges
4	lemons
2	yeast cakes
4	lbs. sugar

Scald the blossoms in the boiling water and let stand overnight. The next morning, strain, add the pulp and juice of 6 oranges, the juice of 4 lemons, the yeast, and the sugar. Let ferment for 4 days, then strain and bottle. Serve in small glasses at room temperature.

Dorde writes, "It seems that with this short period of fermentation, this would be one of your 'slightly alcoholic' beverages."

Thomas Tucker contributed the following old German recipe, which varies slightly from those given above.

German Dandelion Wine

6	cups dandelion petals
2	cups sugar
1	lb. raisins
1	tsp. acid blend
1	gallon hot water
1/4	tsp. tannin
1	pkg. active dry yeast

Cut up raisins and put all ingredients except the yeast into a crock or enamelled or plastic bucket. Pour hot water over ingredients and stir until sugar is dissolved. Set to cool to 70°. Add yeast. Ferment for 3 days covered with a plastic sheet. Siphon into gallon jug and put fermentation lock on. Wine will be ready to rack in 3 weeks. When wine is clear and stable, bottle. Wait for 6 months before drinking.

Emma Byler, an Old-Order Amish herbalist and author of *Plain and Happy Living — Amish Recipes and Remedies* (1992), shared her father's recipe for making and using dandelion wine.

Each spring, Dad would always make up a batch of dandelion wine. This wine was used only for medicinal purposes, such as for hot toddies and so on. I do not remember what it was supposed to cure, but he would fill a bottle or jar with the wine, add his own blend of roots and berries, and drink a shot glass of it each day as a tonic against all sorts of ills. The wine recipe is as follows:

3 1/2	quarts yellow blossoms with the stems removed
1	gallon water
3	lbs. granulated sugar
1	lemon
1	orange
1	Tbsp. yeast

Boil blossoms in the water for 1/2 hour. Strain off the blossoms and add sugar to the remaining liquid. Slice and add both lemon and orange; boil for 3 minutes longer. Set mixture aside to cool. When lukewarm, add yeast. Let mixture rise for 2 days in a crock and then skim off pieces of lemon and orange.

Fill jugs, but leave plenty of space. Do not fill too full. DO NOT CORK. Stretch a balloon over the neck of the jug and keep it at room temperature for four months or until the fermentation is completed (when the balloon is no longer inflated). At this point bottle the wine and cork it up tightly.

If your tastes tend toward the exotic, here are three elegant and intriguing beverages which you might like to try:

Dandelion and Ginger Wine

1	gal. dandelion heads
1	gal. boiling water
1	orange
1	lemon
1/2	oz. bruised ginger root
1/2	lb. raisins, minced
4	lbs. light brown sugar
6	oz. cold, strong tea
	yeast
	yeast nutrient

Put the flowers into a container and pour on the water. Stir, cover and leave for 3 days, stirring every day. Strain the liquid into a pan and put in the thinly pared rinds of the orange and lemon and the ginger root. Bring to a boil and simmer for 30 minutes. Put the juices of the orange and lemon, the raisins, and sugar into a container and strain on the liquid. Add the tea and cool the mixture to body temperature. Add the yeast nutrient and sprinkle the yeast on top. Cover and leave in a warm place to ferment for 7 days. Strain the wine into a 1 gallon jar and fit a fermentation lock. Rack as the wine clears and bottle it when fermentation is complete. Leave the wine for 1 year before opening. It should be a clear yellow color with a slightly pungent flavor (Duff, 1982).

Dandelion Mead

3	qts. dandelion petals
4	lbs. honey
2	gals. water
3	Tbsp. fresh lemon juice

1   cup freshly made, strong tea
6   whole cloves
1   stick cinnamon, crushed
2   Tbsp. wine or "organic" dry yeast

Pack the petals, loosely, into a clean crock or plastic pail. Mix the honey with 1/2 gallon water, bring to a boil and boil for 3 minutes. Pour over the dandelion petals. Add the lemon juice, tea, cloves, and cinnamon. Bring the remaining water to a boil and add to the crock. Cool to lukewarm. Soften the yeast in a little lukewarm water and add to the crock. Cover tightly with a sheet of plastic and let stand for 1 week. Strain; return liquid to the crock, cover tightly, and let stand for at least 2 months. Pour into sterilized bottles; cover with a muslin sheet and let stand for 3 days. Cap or cork and try not to drink before 2 months (Crowhurst, 1973).

You can also make your dandelion wine pink by adding raspberries:

Pink Dandelion Wine

2   quarts dandelion petals
2   quarts boiling water
3   lemons
10 oz.   package frozen, sweetened red raspberries
3 1/2   cups sugar
1   cake yeast

Pick dandelion blossoms early in the morning, gathering enough flower heads to make 2 quarts of petals after the stem and green collar at the end of each flower have been snipped off. Rinse the dandelions in cool water before preparing the petals.

Put the petals in a one-gallon stoneware jar and pour boiling water over them. Let stand overnight. In the morning, strain the liquid through cheesecloth, squeezing the flowers to remove all of the juice. Combine the dandelion juice with the strained juice of 3 lemons, red raspberries, and sugar. Bring the mixture to a boil and simmer for 20 minutes. Pour the mixture back into the jar, cool to lukewarm, and add yeast. Stir until the yeast dissolves, cover the jar, and let the mixture ferment for about 10 days, or until it stops hissing. Using filter paper or a double layer of cheesecloth, strain the liquid into a scalded cider jug and let it stand for three days to settle. Then strain the liquid again and put it into clean quart wine bottles with screw-on caps. Let the wine stand until it is still before corking or capping the bottles tightly. Age the wine in the cellar approximately 9 months. Fills three 4/5 wine bottles (Kluger, 1977).

No section on dandelion wine would be complete without Ceaser Simone's recipe, which is reputed to make the best dandelion wine in Vineland, New Jersey, the dandelion growing capital of the world! It was handed down to him by his father, who got it from his father!

This is how Ceaser's nephew, Tom Pontano, tells it:

To make 50 gallons of dandelion wine — for who would want to make less — you will need three bushels of dandelion blooms, two crates of grapefruits, a crate of oranges, a pound of yeast, 150 pounds of sugar and 50 gallons of water. Put it all together and let it work for about three weeks. Pour it off into a new charred oak barrel and age it for a year or two. Then dump in a can (4 - 5 oz.) of Preservol (available from Milan Labs, New York, New York) and leave it set for 30 days. This clears the wine. Then bottle it with 1/4 tsp. ascorbic acid (Vitamin C) per gallon in sterilized bottles and either drink it or store it. Prepared this way, it will store forever and not turn into vinegar.

This is the wine which has been served for many years at Vineland's annual Dandelion Dinner (see page 79).

And when you are done making the wine, and haven't the foggiest idea what to do with it all, you might try this:

Dandelion Wine Pudding with Ladyfingers

6	egg yolks, beaten
6	egg whites, beaten stiff
4	Tbsp. sugar
1	Tbsp. lemon juice
	grated rind of one orange
1	tsp. cornstarch
3/4	cup dandelion wine
6	Tbsp. confectioner's sugar
1	dozen ladyfingers, split

Combine the egg yolks, sugar, lemon juice, and orange rind. Dissolve the cornstarch in part of the wine before adding to the egg yolk mixture. Cook over simmering hot water until thick, stirring constantly. Let cool. Make a meringue by gradually adding the confectioners' sugar to the stiffly beaten egg whites while beating. Place the split ladyfingers in the bottom and around the sides of an ovenproof serving bowl. Pour in the dandelion custard and top with the meringue. Bake in a moderate oven (350°) for about 12 minutes. The peaks of the meringue should just be tipped with brown. Serve with a small glass of dandelion wine to accent the flavor of the pudding. Serves 6 (Kluger, 1984).

This all sort of changes your perception about all those pretty yellow flowers, doesn't it!

Enjoy!

Chapter 8

The Underground
Dandelion
Recipes for Roots

E ver had the sadistic urge to get even with the dandelions which ruin your garden? How about roasting them and drinking their juices....or, imprisoning them in your cellar and periodically tearing them leaf from leaf!....or boiling them in oil and eating them! If you are going to do these things, however, from October through early December is the time.

The English get even with **their** dandelions by harvesting the roots after the first hard freeze when they are full of nutrients and natural sweeteners, and roasting and grinding them as a caffeine-free coffee substitute. This practice is so popular that Symington's instant roasted dandelion root beverage regularly ranks in the top 100 best sellers for Holland and Barrett Health Food Stores (Britain's equivalent to our General Nutrition Centers health food chain).

The French have what may be an even more soul-satisfying process. They bring big, strong dandelion roots inside each winter, store them in the dark and every week or two divest them of their new growth — the tender, blanched and only mildly-bitter greens.

Orientals, however, may be the most ruthless in torturing dandelions. They collect large roots, clean them, cut them in pieces, add water and a bit of soy sauce, and cook them in oil in their woks. Served over rice, it's sadism at its finest.

The preparation of dandelion coffee is an area where, to get a really good product, you must know what you are doing.

Of the many authors who have written about dandelion coffee, several consider it "just like" or "similar" in flavor to real coffee. Others consider it a "good substitute," and still others find it totally unlike real coffee in flavor. A couple of authors find it "weaker than real coffee." Those who found it weak or unlike coffee most likely either collected spring roots, which are almost flavorless, failed to roast the roots long enough, or are real purists with far more sophisticated taste buds than ours. Our experience is that the best is wonderful, the worst unpalatable, and had we gotten the worst as our first experience, it would probably have been the last.

The Yugoslavian researcher Susnik (Hobbs, 1985) is very enthusiastic about roasted dandelion roots as a healthful coffee substitute. Roasting the roots releases their aromatic chemicals and converts the starch inulin to fructose. The result is a flavorful, relaxing beverage free of caffeine and without the bitterness of coffee. According to Susnik, the drink gently stimulates the digestive and eliminative organs, providing "a wonderful rest from the coffee bean which whips the digestive organs with a rush of false energy via the central nervous system, additionally irritating the mucous membranes."

The technique for making dandelion coffee of the highest quality, in the true British tradition, was told by John A. Rohrback, M. Vet. Med., M.R.C.V.S. in *Herbal Review* (Spring, 1981), the journal of the British Herb Society. His instructions are as follows:

- Gather dandelion roots, uncontaminated by chemical fertilizers and/or noxious poisons, in the third autumn of their lives. (See diagram on page 56). If you don't have an uncontaminated source, you may grow dandelions, either from seed, or from transplants. (See page 49 for seed sources). Dandelion crowns, with an inch or so of root attached, may be gathered in country fields and transplanted to your home garden.

- Dig roots, many of which will be 12 inches or longer, deeply with a good sized fork, taking care not to damage them. Remove the soil carefully and completely with water and a nail brush if necessary. Any cut of the raw root allows the loss of white milky sap containing the active principles of the plants, so up to this stage the roots are kept in their full lengths.

- Steaming prevents loss of sap. It can be done in a kitchen utensil designed for the purpose, or in a colander placed in a saucepan of vigorously boiling water and covered with a lid. **If the roots are cut to fit the receptacle immediately before being placed over the boiling water, there will be very little loss of sap. Do not steam too many at once, or the lower ones will be cooked before the roots on top have been**

reached by the steam. They are sufficiently steamed when a cut surface does not exude any sap.

- Cut the steamed roots into lengths of approximately 1/8 inch and put them on plates to air dry. Dry for one or more days, depending on temperature and humidity, until you feel no softness or moisture when breaking the thicker pieces.

- Place the dry roots, in sparse layers, in shallow baking trays in an oven at about 200° C (350-400° F). **Note: most other recipes call for a roasting temperature of 250° F.** Roast until roots reach a darkness corresponding to the flavor you like. A light yellow color gives a mild flavor; a dark color resembling roasted coffee beans will yield a much stronger aroma and flavor. Much information can be gained from the smell emerging from the oven, and this will reduce the need to open the oven door and lose heat.

- When the roots have reached the desired aroma and color, remove them from the oven. The roots swell during roasting and, somewhat surprisingly, emerge from the oven with a moist consistency. They dry within a few minutes and then are ready either for storing or grinding.

- Grind the roasted roots finely in a coffee grinder or food processor. The fine powder tends to absorb moisture, so grind only a few weeks' supply at a time and keep it in an airtight container. Store the remainder of the roasted but unground material in a securely-closed container.

- Other methods of grinding can be used, such as a mortar and pestle, or even by pressing the roots with a base of a bottle, but the resulting material is coarse-grained and so less flavor and substance passes into the beverage.

If this is a bit too involved for you, there is a simpler way. At a minimum, good quality dandelion "coffee" requires, in addition to gathering the roots in autumn or winter, that you:

- Clean the roots thoroughly,

- Cut them into 1" pieces and roast them in a slow (250°) oven for 2-4 hours, turning regularly to roast the roots evenly until they are brittle and chocolate brown clear through;

- Grind them in a blender or coffee grinder and store them in an air-tight container until needed, or grind them just before brewing.

Just as with real coffee, you can make the flavor stronger by roasting the dandelion roots to a darker color. In fact, Michaels (1980) suggests roasting them twice — once in their original state and again after grinding as the "way you achieve a semblance of that double roast continental flavor which makes good strong coffee."

One level, rather than heaping, teaspoon of ground dandelion root prepared this way and put in a tea ball is all that is required to make a "dandy cuppa brew." Some, like me, may prefer even less, so a little can go a long way. If the roots have been gathered several weeks after the first hard freeze, the inulin in them will have been converted to fructose, and no additional sweetening will be needed. I take mine straight and black; my wife prefers hers with some milk.

Any way you cut (or grind) it, dandelion roots make a soothing, mild, healthful, and caffeine-free alternative to coffee. If you choose not to harvest and roast your own roots, you may buy commercially-available roasted roots or instant coffee substitutes from several sources, most of whom import them already roasted from Holland, Belgium, Germany, and Eastern Europe. The list of suppliers is presented on page 50.

It is best to try samples from several suppliers to see which tastes most like coffee before settling on your source. The flavor of samples we have tried from various sources has been uneven in quality. Don't give up if you find the first sample unpleasant. Try others. The health benefits are worth the effort.

The best we have found, as was mentioned in Chapter 4, is **Thuna's Instant Dandylion Blend,** a blend of roasted dandelion root, barley, and rye, which was available only in Canada until we began importing it for the United States market in 1988. It is available from Goosefoot Acres at both wholesale and retail. An order form is at the back of this book.

If you decide to try dandelion coffee and like coffee ice cream, I leave you with a true taste tempter, discovered by our son-in-law who wondered what ice cream would taste like with some instant dandelion coffee added to it. The result was magnificent — a cross, according to friends who have tried it, between coffee and caramel. Add from 1/8 to 1/4 teaspoon (depending on the size of the serving and how strong you like your coffee flavor) of Thuna Instant Dandylion Blend to vanilla or fudge twirl ice cream and stir it in well. Then enjoy.

Dandelion Root Ice Cream can also be made from scratch. Ron Zimmerman, the owner of The Herbfarm Restaurant in Fall City, Washington, contributed the following recipe, which he says "has become one of the favorites served at The Herbfarm. It has a dark cocoa-chocolate flavor that seems at its best eaten in the months when most of the garden is idle."

Herbfarm Roasted Dandelion Root Ice Cream

2 1/2	cups heavy cream
1 1/2	cups half and half
14	Tbsp. sugar
5	egg yolks
35	young (small) dandelion roots or the equivalent in larger roots prepared as noted

Dig dandelion roots with a shovel. Rinse and scrub the roots well to remove all soil, and let them air dry for a day. Roast roots on a baking sheet in a 250° oven for about 2 to 4 hours, or until the roots become brittle and dark coffee colored. Grind the roasted roots in a coffee grinder or food processor fitted with a metal blade.

Prepare the ice cream base by placing cream, half and half and sugar in a medium pot. Bring to a bare simmer, stirring to dissolve sugar. Add roasted dandelion root powder. Maintain heat at a bare simmer, but do not boil. Let the roots steep for 45 minutes. Strain out and discard root material.

To thicken the mix, break up the egg yolks in another pot. Gradually add the warm dandelion root cream. Return to stove. Heat gently and stir until sauce thickens enough to coat the back of the spoon. Strain again, and chill.

Freeze in an ice cream machine according to manufacturer's directions. Alternately, freeze in a metal bowl, break up mixture, place in a food processor fitted with the metal blade, process quickly until smooth and refreeze.

Also from Falls City, Washington, comes the recipe for **Dandy-Doc**, contributed by Eagle Song Randall of the Moon Valley Herb Co. She says that it is modified often, depending on what is on hand and that they use it most often in the winter.

7	oz. dandelion root
10	oz. mixed burdock and chicory root
1 1/2	lb. hard red wheat or barley (hulless variety preferred)
1/4	oz. yellow dock root

"Each item is roasted separately. We roast dark, but I recommend that people roast the herbs the color of the coffee they usually drink," writes Eagle Song.

In addition to making a roasted beverage, dandelion roots may be transplanted into pots or other convenient containers and brought indoors to provide blanched salad greens all winter. Blanching reduces nutrients somewhat but still yields a nutritious product with little of the bitterness of plants grown in the sunlight. It is these blanched leaves which the French find most choice in making their famous gourmet salad, "Pissenlit au lard" (see page 90).

The procedure is as follows:

- Dig the roots before the ground freezes, and trim away all but 1" of the leaves;

- Replant the roots in 10" of moist soil, topped off by 6-8" of sterilized dampened sand or sawdust;

- When the blanched greens show through the top layer in about 2 to 3 weeks, they are ready to harvest for salads.

- After harvesting, recover the roots with topping and wait 3 weeks for the next harvest.

You can achieve the same effect without the sand or saw-dust topping by simply placing the potted roots in a dark room.

If you wish more nutritious greens and don't mind a little bitterness, leave off the sand/sawdust topping. Bob Tubbesing, of Parma, Ohio, pots the roots and puts the pots on a platform built onto a south-facing window in late November. He cuts a mess of greens from these every two weeks or so through January. He then goes out during a thaw, pots up some fresh roots, and harvests from them until the dandelions emerge outdoors in March.

The greens so produced can be used in any of the recipes presented in Chapter 6. Blanched greens, however, are most tasty in the salads.

If the Oriental approach strikes your fancy, this recipe seems to be almost universal for a **Nituke Style Vegetable:**

1   cup dandelion roots, chopped
1   Tbsp. extra virgin olive oil
     small amount of water
     soy sauce
     salt and pepper to taste

Scrub the roots well, then chop them into thin rings. Sautee in 1 Tbsp. oil per cup of roots until golden and soft. Add a little water, salt, and pepper then cover and stew until tender and most of the water has evaporated. Sprinkle with soy sauce and serve over rice.

The roots can also be cut into salads raw or cooked, steamed and served with butter, salt and pepper, or in any number of imaginative ways.

Even though it has been said already in Chapters 2, 4 and 6, it can't be said too often. If you consume too much of any dandelion product before going to bed and are a sound sleeper, you may have to change sheets in the morning. Otherwise, they will serve as an early morning wake up call.

As you close down your garden for the year, try harvesting and using dandelion roots. You'll fulfill your primitive urges and get lots of healthful and tasty benefits in the process.

Chapter 9

References Cited And Selected Other Sources

The following references have been drawn from an overall bibliography on dandelions which is at least four times this size and growing. I am constantly amazed at how many people have written about the useful aspects of dandelions over the years.

Adams, Charlotte. 1971. *The Four Seasons Cookbook.* Ridge Press, Holt, Rinehart and Winston, NY. p. 198.

Anderson, Jean and Elaine Hanna. 1985. *The New Doubleday Cookbook.* Doubleday, NY. pp. 532, 577.

"Aunt Becky". 1977. *Amish Cooking.* Pathway Publishing Corp., Aylmer, Ontario, Canada. p. 46.

Beard, James. 1977. *Theory and Practice of Good Cooking.* Alfred E. Knopf. Reprint 1990, Wing Books. pp. 325-326, 396-397.

Beard, James and Sam Aaron. 1970. *How to Eat Better for Less Money*. Simon and Schuster, NY. pp. 123, 137, 155-56 .

Benoit, Jehane. 1978. *Madame Benoit Cooks at Home*. McGraw-Hill Ryerson, Ltd. NY. pp. 47-48.

Berglund, Berndt and Clarete Bolsby. 1971. *The Edible Wild*. Pagurian Press, Charles Scribner and Son, NY.

Boxer, Arabella, Jocastra Innes, Charlotte Perry-Crook and Lewis Essen. 1984. *Encyclopedia of Herbs, Spices and Flavorings*. Crescent Books, NY.

Brackett, Babette and Maryann Lash. 1975. *The Wild Gourmet*. David R. Godine. Boston, MA.

Brennan, Georgeanne, Isaac Cronin and Charlotte Glenn. 1985. *The New American Vegetable Cookbook*. Aris Books, Berkeley, CA. pp. 47-56, 121, 276-277.

Bricklin, Mark and Sharon S. Ferguson (eds). 1989. *The Natural Healing and Nutrition Annual*, 1989. Rodale Press, Emmaus, PA.

Byler, Emma A. 1992. *Plain and Happy Living — Amish Recipes and Remedies*. Goosefoot Acres Press, Cleveland Heights, OH.

Candler, Teresa Gilardi. 1980. *Vegetables the Italian Way*. McGraw Hill Co., NY. pp. xxv-xxvi, 23, 41-42,

208-209. (Recipes from her family restaurant in Northern Italy).

Claiborne, Craig. 1961. *The Original New York Times Cookbook*. Harper and Row, NY. p. 417.

Comas, Beatrice H. 1979. "Fixing Dandelions, Down East Style" in *The Lewiston (Maine) Daily Sun*, Modern Living Section, May 17 edition.

Committee on National Formulary. 1960. *National Formulary, 11th Edition*. American Pharmaceuticals Association, Washington, D.C. p. 360.

Core, Earl. n.d. "Plants and Animals of the Bible" in *Bible Study Helps, Holy Bible, King James Version*. World Publishing Co., Cleveland, OH.

Crawford, Patricia. 1976. *The Homesteading Recipe Book*. Macmillan Publishing Co., NY. pp. 1-4.

Crowhurst, Adrienne. 1973. *The Weed Cookbook*. Lancer Books, NY.

DiPalma, Carmen. 1981. *Don't Weed Your Garden Cookbook*. J. Brown Productions, Willoughby, OH.

Duff, Gail. 1982. *The Countryside Cookbook*. Van Nostrand, Reinhold Co., NY. pp. 26-30.

Duke, James. 1993. "Eat Your Weedies." *Organic Gardening*, July/August, 1993.

Duke, James. 1989. "The Synthetic Silver Bullet vs. the Herbal Shotgun." *Herbalgram* No. 18/19: 12-13. P.O. Box 201660, Austin, TX 78720 (Fall/Winter 88-89).

Dunn, Priscilla Hastings. 1977. "Wild Dandelion Greens a Sure Sign of Spring." *Christian Science Monitor*, Thursday, May 26. p. 19.

Famularo, Joe and Louise Imperiale. 1993. *Vegetables: Artichokes to Zucchini.* Barrons. pp. 72-73, 207.

Farmer, Fannie Merritt. 1896, revised 1979. *Fannie Farmers Cookbook*, Bantam Books, revised 12th edition, published by arrangement with Alfred Knopf. 1st Bantam edition Sept. 1983.

Fiorilli, Patrick R. n.d. *Dandelion Recipe Book.* City of Vineland, NJ.

Firth, Grace. 1974. *Living the Natural Life.* Simon and Schuster, NY. pp. 82-83, 176.

Fulweiler, Megan. n.d. "The Edible Dandelion." *Farmstead Magazine*, pp. 54-55.

Gerras, Charles, ed. 1984. *Rodale's Basic Natural Foods Cookbook.* Rodale Press, Inc., Emmaus, PA. pp. 198-203, 737-740.

Good, Frank. n.d. "Think Dandelions are a Pest? It's Good for your Health." *Ridder News Service.*

Gorman, Judy. 1986. *Judy Gorman's Vegetable Cookbook.* Yankee Publishing, Inc., NH. pp. 139-140, 285-2-86, 318-320.

Greene, Bert. 1984. *Greene on Greens.* Workman Publishing Company, Inc. NY. pp. 189-196.

Grieve, Maude. 1937. *A Modern Herbal.* Harcourt Brace. 1971 Reprinted by Dover Publications, NY.

Gruchawka, Peter. 1989. Personal Communication.

Haley, Pat. 1986. *The Nine Seasons Cookbook.* Yankee Publishing Inc. Dublin, NH. pp. 62-67.

Hampstead, Marilyn, owner of Fox Hill Farms, Parma, MI. June, 1988. Personal Communication at International Herb Growers and Marketers Association Meeting, Baton Rouge, LA.

Hanle, Zack. 1971. *Cooking with Flowers.* Price, Stern, Sloan Publishers, Los Angeles, CA.

Harris, Ben Charles. 1961. *Eat the Weeds.* Keats Publishing Co., New Caanan, CT.

Hawkes, Alex D. 1968, Revised 1984. *A World of Vegetable Cookery.* An Encyclopedic Treasury of recipes, botany and lore of the vegetable kingdom. Simon and Schuster, NY. pp. 101-102.

Haytowitz, David B. and Ruth Matthews. 1984. *Composition of Foods: Vegetables and Vegetable Products.* U.S. Department of Agriculture Human Nutrition

Information Service. Agricultural Handbook No. 8-11.

Hazelton, Nika. 1976. *The Unabridged Vegetable Cookbook.* J.B. Lippincott Company, PA. pp. 132-133, 160-161, 286, 311-312.

Hill, Judith and Judith Sutton. 1986. *Cook's Free-Style Cuisine.* Simon and Schuster, NY. p 54. Recipes from Cook's Magazine.

Hobbs, Christopher. 1985. *Monograph on Taraxacum Officinale* Weber. Eclectic Institute, 14385 S.E. Lusted Road, Sandy, Oregon 97055 (503) 668-4120

Hoge, Tom. 1977. "Flavorful Salad of Tender Dandelions." Associated Press Newsfeature.

Hughes-Gilbey, Ann. 1983. *French Country Kitchen.* Chartwell Books, Inc. Secaucus, NJ. p. 100.

Jerome, Carl. 1993. *Cooking for a New Earth.* Henry Holt and Co., NY. p. 171.

Kennedy, Diana. 1978. *Recipes from the Regional Cooks of Mexico.* Harper & Row Publishers, Inc. NY. pp. 54-55.

Kluger, Marilyn. 1984. *The Wild Flavor.* Jeremy P. Tarcher, Inc., Los Angeles, CA. pp. 13, 62-63, 72-73, 76-77, 80-85, 88.

Kluger, Marilyn. 1977. *The Dandelion — A Wonderful Weed with Dozens of Uses.* OFA, pp. 72-75.

Knutsen, Karl. 1975. *Wild Plants You Can Eat.* Doubleday & Co., Inc., Garden City, NY. pp. 32-35.

Kraus, Sibella. 1993. *Greens: A Country Garden Cookbook.* Collins Publishers, San Francisco, CA. p. 66.

Larkcom, Joy. n.d. *The Salad Garden.* Published in cooperation with the New York Botanical Garden Institute of Urban Horticulture by Viking Press, NY. pp. 18, 51-52, 87, 136, 141, 145-146, 152-155.

Lau, Mary Louise. 1977. *The Delicious World of Raw Foods.* Rawson Associates Publishers, Inc., NY. pp. 150-156.

L'Etoila, Valerie Ann, Monique Maine, and Madeline Peter. 1985 (English), 1982 (French). *La Cuisine, A Complete Book of French Cooking.* Gallery Books, NY.

Leroy, Ph. and Y. Jannes (Translated by R. F. Fullick.). 1981. *The Elle Cookbook.* Mermaid Books, Michale Joseph LTD, London. p. 125.

McPherson, Alan and Sue McPherson. n.d. *Edible and Useful Wild Plants of the Urban West.* Pruitt Publishing Co., Boulder, CO.

Mahnken, Jan. 1985. *A Cook's Garden.* Countryman Press, Woodstock VT. pp. 20, 41, 43, 48.

Marcus, George and Nancy. 1982. *Forbidden Fruits and Forgotten Vegetables*. St. Martin's Press, NY.

Marter, Marilynn. 1977. "Don't Kill the Weeds, Eat Your Dandelions." *Pasadena (CA) Star News* p. C-7, April 20.

Maynard, Kitty and Lucian Maynard. 1990. *The American Country Inn Bed and Breakfast Cookbook, Vol. 2.* Rutledge Hill Press, Nashville, TN. p. 520.

Michael, Pamela. 1980. *All Good Things Around Us.* Holt, Rinehart, Winston, NY.

Miller, Ann. n.d. *Organic Annie's Wild Food Delights*, 2600 Conners Road, Baldwinsville, NY 13027 (315) 638-2729.

Miller, Mrs. Joe L. 1983. "Dandelion Jelly" in "Cooking with Maudie," *The Budget*, Sugarcreek, OH. May 11.

Minnich, Jerry. 1983. *Gardening for Maximum Nutrition.* Rodale Press, Emmaus, PA. pp. 70-71, 159, 200-201.

Morash, Marian. 1982. *The Victory Garden Cookbook.* Alfred Knopf, NY. pp. 244-252.

Morash, Marian. 1993. *The Victory Garden Fish and Vegetable Cookbook.* Alfred Knopf, NY. pp. 57-58, 94.

Nyerges, Christopher. 1982. *Wild Greens and Salads*. Stackpole Books, Harrisburg, PA. pp. 67-72.

O'Ceirin, Cyril and Kit O'Ceirin. 1978. *Wild and Free: Cooking From Nature*. Skilton and Shaw, London.

Owen, Millie. 1984. *A Cook's Guide to Growing Herbs, Greens and Aromatics*. Alfred Knopf, NY. pp. 100-104.

Palazzi, Antonella. 1991. *The Great Book of Vegetables*. Simon and Schuster, NY. p. 58.

Philips, Roger. 1986. *Wild Foods*. Little, Brown and Co. p. 33.

Pontano, Tom. 1989. Dandelion grower in Vineland, NJ. Personal Communication.

Rombauer, Irma S. and Marion Rombauer Becker. 1975. *Joy of Cooking*. Bobbs-Merrill Co, Indianapolis, IN. p. 94.

Root, Waverley. 1980. *Food*. Simon and Schuster, NY. pp. 102-103.

Schneider, Elizabeth. 1985. "Great Greens! A New Appreciation for Delicious Down-Home Vegetables" in *Food and Wine*. October. pp. 71-75, 97-99.

Schneider, Elizabeth. 1986. *Uncommon Fruits & Vegetables. A Common Sense Guide*. Harper & Row. pp. 162-166.

Schwartz, Leonard. 1992. *Salads*. Harper Perennial, NY. pp. 68-69, 144-145.

The Settlement Cookbook Company. 1965. *The Settlement Cookbook*. Simon and Schuster, NY. p. 396.

Silverman, Maida. 1977. *A City Herbal*. Alfred Knopf, NY.

Smith, Jeff. 1984. *The Frugal Gourmet*. Ballantine Books, pp. 56-57.

Smith, Jeff and Craig Wollam. 1991. *The Frugal Gourmet Culinary Handbook*. Wm. Morrow Co. pp. 203-204, 416.

Squier, Tom. 1989. "Living Off the Land." *Moore County Citizen News Record*. April 12, p. 7.

Sunset Books. 1983. *Sunset Vegetable Cookbook*. Lane Publishing Co., Menlo Park, CA. pp. 8-9.

Sunset Books, eds. 1987. *Fresh Produce A to Z; How to Select, Store and Prepare*. Lane Publishing Co., Menlo Park, CA. pp. 83-85.

Tierra, Michael. 1983. *The Way of Herbs*. Washington Square Press, NY. pp.15-16, 41,45-46, 121-122.

Time-Life Books, eds. 1980. *The Good Cook. Techniques and Recipes for Salads*. Time-Life Books, Inc. NY. pp. 36-37, 124.

University of California — Berkeley, School of Public Health. 1990. *Wellness Letter*. Berkley, CA, February.

Verolzheimer, Ruth (ed). 1976, revised 1986. *Culinary Arts Institute Encyclopedic Cookbook, New Revised Edition*. G. P. Putnam's Sons, NY. pp. 22, 34, 282, 920.

Vilmorin-Andrieux, M.M. n.d. *The Vegetable Garden*. Ten Speed Press, CA. pp. 228-230.

Wells, W.S. & Son. n.d. *Fiddleheads, Beet Greens and Dandelion Greens*. W.S. Wells & Sons, Wilton, ME.

Whitman, Joan (compiler). 1985. *Craig Claiborne's New York Times Food Encyclopedia*. Time Books, NY. p. 133.

Witt, Reni. L. 1983. *PMS - What Every Woman Should Know about Premenstrual Syndrome*. Stein and Day, Scarsborough House, NY. p. 187.

Zelienka, R. D. and E.F. Yoder. 1986. *From Heart to Hearth—Selections of Amish Recipes and Folklore*. Especially for You Publishing Co., Coloma, WI. pp. 36, 62, 145.

Index

AVAILABLE FROM GOOSEFOOT ACRES

The Little Known Treasures of Northeastern Ohio Map Book A compilation of fascinating, mostly word-of-mouth ethnic and elegant treasures which enrich the landscape and townscapes of Northeastern Ohio. Nine detailed maps. **By Peter A. Gail, Ph.D., 60 pages, 8 1/2 x 11 spiral bound** **$6.50**

Plain & Happy Living — Amish Recipes and Remedies Autobiography and folk medicine handbook of an Old Order Amish woman widowed at age 33 with 10 children. Herbal remedies, recipes for household products and delicious foods on a very low budget, interwoven with wonderfully warm stories and anecdotes. **By Emma Byler, 160 pages, 21 illus., 6 x 9 paperback (ISBN 1-879863-71-5)** **$9.95**

Lessons of the Amish Lifestyle — An Introduction with a Focus on Education The Amish have much to teach us about practical economics, raising children and self-sufficient living. This little book introduces their culture and focuses on how the Amish raise children which can be adapted to non-Amish society. **By Peter A. Gail, Ph.D., 34 pages, 5 1/2 x 8 1/2 saddle stitched** **$3.50**

The Dandelion Celebration — A Guide to Unexpected Cuisine What's the best thing to do about your dandelions? EAT THEM! Discover the history and nutritional and medicinal properties of this lawnscaping arch villain as you learn how to pick, prepare, and savor every part of the plant! **By Peter A. Gail, Ph.D., 160 pages, 9 photos, 5 1/2 x 8 1/2 paperback (ISBN 1-879863-51-0)** **$10.95**

Goosefoot Acres Volunteer Vegetable Sampler Growing weeds for food is a $5 million a year industry! Stop wasting good vegetables. Recipes for and facts about 15 common backyard weeds, plus a curriculum unit which introduces children to the culinary marvels of the dandelion. **By Peter A. Gail, Ph.D., 90 pages, 8 1/2 x 11 spiral bound** **$8.00**

The Delightful Delicious Daylily Recipes for "tubers," shoots, buds, flowers, and fruits of the daylily, plus plant history and cultivation. Includes sources of further information on the daylily for serious enthusiasts. **By Peter A. Gail, Ph.D., 50 pages, 5 1/2 x 8 1/2 spiral bound** **$5.00**

Thuna Instant Dandylion Blend Delicious instant roasted beverage made from extracts of roasted dandelion root, barley and rye. Tastes similar to coffee but without caffeine. Naturally sweetened with its own fructose. **2.8 oz. (80 gm.) container makes 70-100 cups (6 - 8 cents a cup!)** Imported from Canada. Write for separate brochure. **$5.95**

ORDER FORM

Name: _____
Address: _____
City/State: _____ Zip _____
Telephone: (____) _____ Date: _____

QUAN-TITY	TITLE/ PRODUCT DESCRIPTION	COST PER ITEM*	TOTAL

*Prices subject to change without notice. Please enclose check or money order with order slip. Make checks payable to GOOSEFOOT ACRES, INC. **DO NOT SEND CASH.** Ohio residents add 7% sales tax. SHIPPING: Please add $3.50 for the first item ordered and $1.00 for each additional item.	**SUB-TOTAL:**
	SALES TAX:
Please bill my VISA/MASTERCARD: Acct. No. _____	**SHIP-PING:**
Expiration Date _____ Signature _____	**TOTAL DUE:**

SHIP TO: (If different than above)
Name: _____
Address: _____
City/State: _____ Zip _____

MAIL THIS ORDER FORM AND PAYMENT TO:
Goosefoot Acres, Inc.,
P. O. Box 18016, Cleveland, Ohio 44118
QUESTIONS? Call (216) 932-2145
CREDIT CARD ORDERS BY PHONE: (800) 697-4858